THE PURSUIT OF
SOCIAL
BUSINESS
EXCELLENCE

Vala Afshar & Brad Martin

Published by Charles Pinot

First Printing, 2012
10 9 8 7 6 5 4 3 2 1

Material in this book is for educational purposes only. This product is sold with the understanding that neither any of the authors nor the publisher are engaged in rendering legal, accounting, investment, or any other professional service specifically suited to one particular individual's needs who may be reading this book. Neither the publisher nor the authors assume any liability for any errors or omissions or for how this book or its contents are used or interpreted or for any consequences resulting directly or indirectly from the use of this book.

The views expressed by the individuals in this book do not necessarily reflect the views shared by the companies they are employed by (or the companies mentioned in this book). The employment status and affiliations of the authors with the companies referenced are subject to change.

Table of Contents

DEDICATIONS

Vala Afshar

To my better half and lifelong soul mate, Stacey – all that I am and will be is because of your inspiration and support. You give more than you receive, and you do it because you care more than others can possibly imagine. You are my greatest find and you will always be the co-author of my life's story.

Donya, Pari, and little Vala, you are my life's purpose.

To my father, James – I will do my very best to become a fraction of the man that you are. You are the hardest working, most unselfish and giving man. You are my hero. To my mother, Showkat – you are the strongest, most courageous and loving person in my life. I am who I am because of the both of you. On behalf of my sister Val, I thank you for your unconditional love, and all the sacrifices you both have made to make our lives better. I love you both.

To my colleagues at Enterasys and to my team, as Isaac Newton famously said, "If I have seen further it is by standing on the shoulders of giants." Brian Townsend, Michael Lytle, Steve Kelly, Ian Miles, Heribert Rehart, Robert Cruz, Yvon Girard, and Michael Lam, thank you for lending me your shoulders.

To my mentor and leader, Chris Crowell, thank you for your shared wisdom, generosity, and confidence in me. I am grateful for the opportunity to stand beside you as we continue to build and grow our company.

Brad Martin

To my amazing wife Rachel and the best three kids I could ask for, Olivia, Ethan and Hazel. You are my inspiration and my motivation.

To my parents Bruce and Renie who have always inspired me to exceed my goals and be a better person. To my siblings, Jessica and Luke who have been mentors and leaders in my life.

To all of my teams and colleagues at Enterasys Networks with whom I have grown and nurtured a great business and community.

To my boss and friend Chris Crowell who has provided me with learning opportunities, great leadership guidance and inspired many of the advancements in this book.

From Vala and Brad

The pursuit of social excellence is a way of life and the journey begins at home. Live a recommendable life and be grateful for all that you have. Appreciate the people that are committed to helping you succeed. Learn to reciprocate with vigor and resolve. It is the generosity and support of others that shapes who we are and what we can achieve.

We sincerely hope that you enjoy reading our story. We greatly appreciate your feedback and support. We will always make ourselves available to you to the best of our ability. When one teaches, two learn. To that end, please visit our web site to further your pursuit of social business excellence:

www.socialbusinessexcellence.com

We wish you the very best of luck with your pursuit of social business excellence.

Vala and Brad

Twitter contacts: @ValaAfshar and @Brad_W_Martin

INTRODUCTION

The "Why" Matters

Why do underdogs win?

As business leaders, we work hard every day to help ensure the success of our company. We know that it feels good to win; it feels better to win as a team; and it feels best to share our successes with customers and business partners. In today's social era, businesses can successfully extend their core beliefs and guiding principles to employees, customers, and partners. In order to achieve success, companies must cultivate a culture of courage, transparency, meritocracy, openness, and shared accountability. The most important foundational elements for successful social transformation are a company's culture and its people.

In this social and mobile era, customers have choices and voices that are scaled and amplified like never before. For businesses to truly connect with our employees and customers we must be able to listen, respond, engage, and add value in a timely and robust manner. But to truly connect, we must do so by way of a personalized and mutually beneficial approach; and in order to do this well, we must embrace social collaboration.

Transformation to a social business is not a technological journey, but rather a cultural, people-oriented, and process-driven pursuit. Businesses must find a way to move from transaction-based mentalities to being engagement oriented. Our employees and customers want to know where we are going, and why; people want to know what we believe in. In this social era, connecting to likeminded organizations is a growth driver.

"People don't buy what you do; people buy why you do it." - @SimonSinek

As leaders at Enterasys Networks, we have made a conscious decision to shift away from talking about what we do and how we do it, to instead talking about what we believe in. It all started with our company ethos: "There is nothing more important than our customers." We believe that companies must consistently deliver on their promises and embrace shared accountability in an open and trusting manner. But our definition of 'customer' is not limited to people that are outside of our company.

Anytime we deliver a service to a recipient, whether she is on the inside or outside of our company, we consider that recipient to be 'our customer'. We all have the opportunity to service others within the enterprise, and thus we all have direct customers regardless of our function in the company. Our social business transformation was seeded with the core tenet that in order to establish trust, we must clearly display competence and intentions. Our intentions, defined by our 'customers first' ethos, have established a company-wide culture that includes a unified commitment to serve with dignity, passion, respect, and inclusiveness. We must also appreciate and work hard to consistently deliver on our promises: competence is shaped by reliability. A social business simply cares more; a social business lives its culture. Authenticity is found at the intersection of what we believe, what we say, and what we do. A social business is, above all, authentic.

"Change almost never fails because it's too early. It almost always fails because it's too late." - @ThisIsSethsBlog

In today's hyper-connected social and mobile era, a business must be able to change and adapt in order to achieve sustainable growth. The market is the wind, and we cannot control the wind. But we can work to ensure the wind is blowing behind our backs. To that end, we must recognize that social and mobile initiatives are no longer a technology discussion, but are instead a lifestyle. Today's mobile and social lifestyle has seen an unprecedented scale and velocity of adoption by our customers and employees. The positive business impact of social and mobile technologies is no longer questionable. Those who fail to use these technologies are either out of business already, or they are on their way out.

"You may hate gravity, but gravity does not care." - @ClayChristensen

Substitute "gravity" with "social collaboration" and "mobility" in the above quote, and the sentiment will stay true. So, what are the steps to take if you have been tasked with transforming your business to embrace social collaboration? What are the foundational elements for a successful and sustainable social business transformation?

If you think that social business transformation is mostly about acquiring the right technology, you're seriously underestimating the foundational elements that your company will need before technology is a factor. Successful social business transformation is led first by culture, people, process, and lastly technology. Every business needs a mantra, guiding principles to ensure purposeful and ethos-aligned communication. A meaningful purpose is crucial to driving business transformation.

"Communication is everyone's panacea for everything." - @Tom_Peters

Effective and purposeful communication in business is the catalyst behind social collaboration. After reading this book, you will be able to leverage the experiences we've had at our company in order to better understand and communicate the power of social networking in your own business, and we are confident that you will be able to answer and address the following commonly asked questions about this new journey in social collaboration:

1. What is a social business and why is it important?

2. How can you maximize your ability to compete, win, and expand market share in the social era by leveraging social collaboration principles?

3. What are the foundational organizational elements needed to ensure a successful social business transformation?

4. How can you scale your company's brand using social collaboration?

5.   How can you delight your customers and achieve world-class customer loyalty and commitment?

6.   How can social collaboration help build a culture of internal advocacy that leads to external influence?

7.   What is the impact of social collaboration on research, development, as well as "blue ocean" innovation?

8.   Can social collaboration transform an organization from a defensive to an offensive preemptive service delivery model?

9.   Can social collaboration accelerate co-creation and adoption of the best practices across business lines?

10. What are the best examples of social selling and marketing with hard return of investment (ROI)?

11. How important is an integrated social customer relationship management (CRM) framework to a successful social collaboration strategy?

12. What is the future of social business and how will it affect customer service, engineering, sales, human resources, and other key functions?

We are not industry analysts. We are not technology futurists, pundits, social innovation experts, ninjas, or gurus. But, we have been the first company to invent multi-industry, award-winning, patent-pending technology that enables our customers to communicate with machines via social networks. We have leveraged social technologies to build world-class product engineering, and customer service organizations. Industry analysts, and the press, have also recognized us for quality differentiation when it comes to our products and services.

This book is our business story. We won't talk much about other companies, management practices, or future technology trends that don't apply to the work we are doing at Enterasys. We purposefully avoid referencing outside studies, because our intent is not to compare and contrast our approach with other implementations of similar practices. This book was written with the sole purpose to share our own success story with you. Some portions of our story may be controversial and subject to scrutiny, but the facts are, we are managing award-winning organizations that outpace the market, we are growing faster than most of our competition, and we were recognized as Boston's "Best Place to Work 2012."

We are winning, and we're proud to be leading an organization that outperforms the market based on our customer-focused ethos. We've achieved successful growth by intentionally and meticulously transforming our business into a social organization, and we are confident that our story will guide you on your own transformation journey in social business. Let's do this, together.

So why do underdogs win? Underdogs win because they know they can.

Twitter Takeaways

A social business cultivates a culture of courage, transparency, meritocracy, openness, and shared accountability.

A social business nurtures connections with employees and customers by adopting a listening and learning culture.

A social business must consistently deliver on their promises, and embrace shared accountability and value co-creation.

Social business transformation is led first by culture, people, process and lastly technology. Social is a mindset.

In order to establish trust, you must clearly display competence and intentions. Without trust, there is no influence.

A social business is commitment to serve with dignity, passion, respect, and inclusiveness.

Competence is shaped by reliability.

A social business simply cares more.

A social business lives its culture, authentically - visible alignment of what we believe, say and do.

Why do underdogs win?   Underdogs win because they know they can.

CHAPTER ONE:

Lead with Purpose

Good Business is Personal

Historically when you read the word "social" to define a business, you think "charitable," but there is a new definition of Social Enterprise gaining ground, and now is the time for forward-thinking companies to adopt it wholeheartedly. Social businesses know how to compete, win, and expand in a competitive market by relying on the collaboration of their employees, executives, partners, and customers. A social business operates with the guiding principle that each employee's responsibility is to serve one other, and that those we serve, even internally, are our customers. To earn internal customer trust and loyalty, each employee must be dependable, available, responsive, and committed to the success of the whole. Success on the outside depends on our ability to execute on the inside.

In a social business, employee communication must be fast, efficient, and personal. For this reason, traditional business communication mediums such as corporate intranets, email, instant messaging, and faxing are being augmented or replaced with social collaboration tools. Today, the most efficient companies use internal and external social media tools to expand their reach, bolster their execution, and promote transparency through the entire company. Transparency in business is authentic, clear and frequent communication of our beliefs and intentions with respect to desired direction and destination. No longer does a traditional hierarchical model or a "need to know basis" mentality work for a modern company. Utilizing mass communication within your business is the singular key to your business' success.

The pursuit of social business excellence is the pursuit of effective mass collaboration. This is a book about collaboration. Successful large-scale collaboration consists of delivering quality content and context, in a timely and compelling manner, to customers, partners, and employees. When you are able to communicate with authenticity and scale—extending the voice of your employees within the company-wide ecosystem, inside and outside of your business—then you have achieved "social business excellence."

In the chapters to come, we will show you what we did within our own company to achieve award-winning results that have been recognized throughout the industry. Our goal is to teach you how to compete, win, and expand your reach using collaboration built on current and emerging technologies.

Our story will begin with an emphasis on the key building blocks that enable social business transformation. We will explicitly list step-by-step procedures for you to follow. We will also specify exact implementation practices and corresponding ROI metrics. Once we have successfully defined the foundational elements of a social business, we will begin discussing social implementation case studies. We will start with basic social technology and procedural practices. Following this we will shift gears to share with you examples of advanced, industry-first innovation that is a few years ahead of today's market. Depending on the maturity level of your organization, you can decide how far you want to take this. At our company, it has taken six years to build and cultivate this foundation. For us it is only the beginning.

Social is a Mindset

Social collaboration is not just about social media, tools, lean processes, and management methodologies. Social collaboration is a mindset that leverages culture, people, process, and technology to unlock the full potential of the organization. The social mindset's ultimate goals are business agility and customer delight. To stay relevant, business leaders must learn strategies, techniques, and social collaboration methodologies relevant to the modern day enterprise; they must figure out how to discover stakeholder value, and provide bottom-line business results. We will describe our social transformation philosophy and methodology with specific examples that positively impacted our business. More importantly, we'll emphasize the factors that have been critical to our success in order of importance.

It may be surprising to hear that two technologists, working for a technology company, serving highly savvy customers and partners, list "technology" as the least significant element for a successful social business transformation; but we strongly believe that it's not the tools themselves, or knowing how to use them, that matter; it's the social ethos of your business. Aside from social media and technological know-how, you will need to adopt transparency in your business, position key people into place, establish a vibrant culture, and implement streamlined processes, flatten reporting structures and pragmatic technology.

"Social" is a mindset. We often use the words "collaboration" and "social" interchangeably. "Social" is not just about social media; we like to think of "social" as "collaboration that is driven by a purpose." For us, the purpose is that there's nothing more important than our customers. We figured out very early on that if you can't deliver excellence to your internal customers, you will be unable to deliver excellence to your external customers. We introduced the idea of internal customers in the beginning of this book. But let's expand this idea: your sales organization is a customer to your service organization, your engineering organization is a customer to your sales organization, and your marketing organization is a customer to your sales operation, and so on. A modern enterprise must have different lines of business working collaboratively under one roof. Thus it is important to creating a transparent, collaborative ecosystem, which knows and appreciates the fact that "no one of us is as smart as all of us."

When we discuss various disciplines and functions in a collaborative organization, we're talking less about departments and more about processes. In a social business, customer service and support is not viewed as a department, but rather as a process where every stakeholder—meaning every employee—is empowered to delight the customer. When all of your internal departments respect each other and strive to win together, you are on the right track. You can fail alone, but in order to win, you need to work together. It is the collaborative bond, united by the common purpose of delighting customers, which fuels company success. Enterasys is a great example of this; it is our collaborative mindset that fuels our growth and passion to serve.

We begin this book with asking the question "Why do underdogs win?" While we have made mention of the word "underdog," we don't really like it because of its negative connotations. Enterasys doesn't have a well-known public brand, and yet we compete against very strong companies with enormous brands... and we win. We win because we have built our business on three pillars of success:

1. Product quality
2. Customer service and support
3. Pragmatic innovation

We put "product quality" first because if the product doesn't work, we simply can't compete and win. Buyer's remorse will make the customer question why they decided to go with our product in the first place. Every product has potential for improvements or defects. So, "strong customer service and support" is the next important pillar of our success. The authors of this book are responsible, respectively, for global product quality and global service quality at Enterasys. This brings us to the third pillar. We believe that small to medium size organizations must embrace innovation as a way to outsmart larger competitors. At a startup, or smaller to mid-size companies, outworking larger competitors is not a viable and sustainable growth strategy. At our company, for every one of our employees, our largest competitor has sixty-five. For this reason alone we have to leverage better processes, enabled by smart use of technology, to bolster our execution speed in order to differentiate ourselves and compete.

The use of social technology is the way we have chosen to scale our company's reach, and how we increased the visibility of interdependencies across our different lines of business. Through the use of social technologies, our ability to scale shared accountability and measure results across functional boundaries allows our organization to maintain forward momentum. One of the main advantages of social business transformation is the acceleration of business agility gained through mass collaboration.

Respecting Your Internal Customers

As we've mentioned, in order to delight our external customers, we had to first learn to delight our internal customers. Here's an example of a common scenario that shows how interconnected our various organizations are at Enterasys:

When an external customer contacts our service organization about a product issue, the service organization follows through by engaging, documenting, analyzing, and reporting their findings to various other functions within Enterasys. In scenarios where analysis uncovers a product defect, feature enhancements can be achieved. The service organization then relies on internal dependencies in other disciplines—such as research & development, product engineering, and marketing—to deliver a final resolution to the customer.

Often, a customer contact lifecycle requires the input and involvement of multiple stakeholders across multiple lines of business within our organization. Please remember, customer experience is simply a collection of memories. In order for each customer engagement to result in a positive memory, many people from different organizations are collaborating behind the scenes to achieve a common goal. Any time you are tasked with delivering a service, the recipient on the other end is your customer. As in the scenario above, customer service and support is the customer of engineering because a dependency exists between the two organizations.

In any business, there are incredible amounts of diverse interdependencies across multiple disciplines with both geographical and functional constraints and variations. It's not enough to be collaborative and work nicely together if you can't deliver a deadline. Discipline, transparency, and adherence to service level agreements drive the culture of accountability in a social business. It is easy and comfortable to say you're accountable, but unless you measure the results of your performance and are willing to share the outcome with subordinates and peers outside of your line of business, you do not have true transparency.

During more challenging times, collaboration is particularly noteworthy. Some organizations are willing to collaborate only if the communication filters out "the bad stuff." Unfortunately, in order to establish trust, we must have the courage to communicate our mistakes and losses too. We must accept that the pursuit of perfection can prevent us from delivering timely value to our customers. A more healthy strategy is one that is agile and infused with a spirit that strives for continuous improvement. In a social business, organizations boastfully talk about learning from their mistakes and they consistently share the good, the bad, and the ugly. Only communicating perfection and achievement is not representative of real life and real work. To be social, you must also be transparent.

In business, we are all aware and respectful of the external customer who is paying for the services or goods. But some companies can lose sight of their internal customers, who are just as important. An awareness of and respect for internal customers is crucial in order to have a business that works properly; and a business that works properly has layers of accountability, openness, cross-functional cooperation, and constructive change. When we treat our internal customers like external customers, we start to gain these qualities, and break down barriers.

At our company, we went through an internal cultural redefinition during which we defined explicitly how we wanted people to act. (We'll talk more about this in Chapter 3.) Our cultural initiative was focused on building a social fabric of cross-functional cooperation, and encouraging all of our employees to share constructive feedback without being defensive. This required a practiced ethos of working together, where everyone rows the same boat in the same direction. A social business has a heightened sense of awareness of cultural drift. Resource alignment accelerates a company's ability to execute and win.

Lead, Follow, or Get Out of the Way

Later in this book we'll cover the foundational elements of successful adoption of social collaboration in order of their importance: culture, people, strategy, process, structure, and technology. We will also provide you with a step-by-step process to help you develop your own company's transformational blueprint. We emphasize technology as the last step you will need in order to become a social business. Based on our experience (and it's been a great experience) business growth and success is not about social technologies. Rather, it is a mindset and value system that embraces and is enabled by technology, but is not defined by it.

Social business transformation starts with culture. You must have a purpose that's meaningful and relevant to your market, customers, and employees. In business, and life, every person has three choices: lead, follow, or get out of the way. If you want your employees to lead and follow, you have to clearly articulate a direction and destination that's meaningful to them. As humans, we feel a need to contribute. Nobody gets up in the morning and says "I can't wait to be mediocre today." Everybody comes to work hoping that they can move the needle. Some do, and some don't. Culture is ultimately what happens when the manager leaves the room. For a business to thrive and stay vibrant, management must tell employees and customers where they're going, and why.

Another way of characterizing people is this: you have thinkers, doers, and watchers. In a social business, you can see the powerful combination of the thinkers and doers who rise to the top. At the same time, you can also pick out the watchers, who are less effective. Collaborators are standing in the front sharing their thoughts, accomplishments, and locating potential obstacles that might impede success. Conversely, watchers sit on the sidelines. In a social business, you can't simultaneously be a watcher and be a part of the team. In a social business that strives for transparency and accountability, everyone is expected to make tough decisions to serve the best interest of the customer.

A social business is still a business; a business that has a laser-sharp focus on revenue, profit, market share, and all the other key traditional factors related to business success. A social business leverages the genius of the crowd in order to achieve its success.

With a social business, you get the inside advantage of being able to see the early signs of potential drift from the cultural attributes that make a winning team. In order to identify drift, you must first baseline what your desired culture looks like. At Enterasys, we determined that the most impactful way to define, own, and advocate would be to have the employees of our company collectively contribute to this process. The result of this mass collaboration led to a company "culture card" that was built by the people and for the people, with very little oversight from senior leadership.

For us, culture is indicative of a business' personality. We engaged our entire company to explicitly define what we wanted our personality to be. This grassroots campaign of capturing our company's personality was a powerful example of a social business approach toward instilling shared accountability, teamwork, and pride in ownership. It was more than just a culture card. It was the fabric that tied our company together, merging our core beliefs and guiding principles together to create a business culture that came from within.

A very important element of maintaining social collaboration momentum in a business is recognizing and rewarding the behavior and outcomes that align with your beliefs and core purpose. As Tom Peters famously said, "Celebrate what you want to see more of." Upon completion of our culture card, our CEO, Chris Crowell, and his entire staff made a strong commitment and show of solidarity by recognizing, celebrating, and communicating their support of the voice of the employees. It was important for Chris, as the leader of our organization, to enthusiastically and passionately support the employees' efforts toward shaping our company culture. Mahatma Gandhi said, "My life is my message." It was Chris' and every employee's mission to ensure we lived our company's message: "There is nothing more important than our customers."

In a social business, the best ideas win, not the best titles. Our culture card represents the best ideas from single contributors who are able to intelligently and compassionately define who we want to be and why. We keep our culture card and elements of it physically visible in our business: it's in our email signatures, on our conference room walls, and on the back of our business cards. It has become such an ingrained part of our company that it's no longer easy to point to one or two contributors who have led the way to defining and instituting our company ethos. Now, it's an indelible part of our business. You see, another attribute of a social business is the notion of a "leader-less" ecosystem, where ideas become actions and are realized through the collective genius of the crowd.

A social business has a flat hierarchy, ultra-clear transparency, and no boundaries between different organizations within the company, thus any individual, at any level, in any function has the ability to rise to the top by demonstrating their leadership abilities. In a social business, cultural alignment and business continuity is key to success. A culture is a business's personality; this is why, at Enterasys, we had the employees of our company work together to define what our personality would be.

In a recent Harvard Business Review post entitled "All Organizations Are Social, But Few Are Social Organizations," Mark P. McDonald poses the following question: "Organizations consist of people. How well an organization works depends on how its people interact and work together. Thus, every organization is 'social.' But so what? How do we make use of this universal fact?" McDonald says that a true social business is not just a traditional hierarchical, vertical interaction of people; what social businesses have is an ability to work across the seams of the business process. They understand the various nuances and interactions that take place within departments and across business lines. We agree with this definition; in fact, the whole social dimension has evolved over time in businesses that live by the concept that the best ideas win, not the best titles. Nothing exemplifies this concept better than the authors of this book: two students, who joined Enterasys Networks as interns while in graduate school, who were given increasing responsibilities, promoted over a dozen times, and ultimately worked their way to the executive level where they report directly to the CEO.

If you produce good work, you're dependable, and you deliver on your promises, you will get more responsibility. Leaders develop future leaders, not future followers. That's the beauty of social collaboration and the power of social media. You can develop a personal brand if you are willing to collaborate, share, learn, and teach others. In a social business, the individual employee has the opportunity to accelerate their career trajectory because they work in a highly dynamic and transparent environment. The opportunity for extended visibility and the dynamic nature of a social business is welcoming for high-producing, highly engaged overachievers. This is especially true for social businesses that also invest in social technologies. To go even further, it helps connect employees with similar interests and objectives in order to establish a community that moves forward together. In a social business, momentum is generated by the individual, but is sustained by the community.

In this social era, the voice of the company is the collective voice of the employees. The brand is a composite of the frontline employees, the managers, the directors… all the way up to the CXOs. Any investment in the employee is an investment in the brand. A social business is, above all else, people-centric.

Technology is Helping Create a Better Social Enterprise

A mantra of a collaborative organization is: "It's not about connecting the dots; it's about connecting the people." Social collaboration is defined by purpose, not by technology. Technology merely enables us to share and collaborate in the most seamless fashion across the enterprise. Businesses have been using technology to communicate for centuries. For many traditional businesses, email is still the most modern form of communication, but for more advanced, collaborative, social organizations, email has become less and less relevant. One of the reasons for this is that email is not as personal, seamless, or lean as other contemporary social mediums. When an email from your CEO goes out to everyone in the company, it lacks the personal touch.

In contrast, using a social interface like Chatter, a social media tool from Salesforce.com, allows for a more personal line of communication. Our CEO regularly chats with the entire company about a variety of topics including sales wins, business strategy, personal stories, industry news, and other compelling updates that help personalize his brand and bolster our company's forward momentum. As he chats, his communication to the employees is formatted to include his picture and bio, which helps personalize his communication. He uses his own words, and people connect to that. A big email list tends to be depersonalizing, whereas Chatter, and other internal social tools like it, make communication more "connectable." Using a tool like Chatter instead of email is a quick and easy way to align your business and expand your thought modeling. Social collaboration establishes a company culture of connectivity and wholeness.

Email is on its way out as the primary way for companies to communicate internally because mass communications lack personable and relatable contextual elements. Gary Vaynerchuck stated, "If content is king, context is god." E-mail often misses the proper context for deep understanding that can lead to meaningful action. If people don't understand the context of the message (if it's not personalized, relevant, and timely) it's just white noise.

Today, business moves at a fast clip. The ecosystem, which includes the hyper-connected employee, customer and business partner, demands availability and support in real time, or as close to it as possible. For this reason, communication must be crisp and timely. The chitchat afforded by social media may appear to lack substance, and in some instances it does, but for normal, non-critical communication, email no longer suffices. Social connectivity fosters bi-directional communication over time, because the social mindset is ultimately humanizing.

It is not uncommon for employees of any company to have had the experience of walking down a company's hallway and passing an executive. Perhaps you have experienced the uncomfortable situation of avoiding eye contact, or not even being addressed by name. This is uncomfortable, right? Today, as executives at our company, we'll walk down the hallways of our campus and our employees will say, "Hi Vala, Hi Brad." ...and we'll say, "Hello. How are you Mary?" We do not need to hastily glance down at a name identification badge in order to be able to respond to a greeting. We recognize and get to know each other through internal social media. This lowers barriers and encourages friendlier in-person interactions within our walls. The purpose of shifting from transactions to engagements is to deepen the connection based on trust, humility, and the willingness to co-create. That's personalization. In a social business, because authentic connections are formed with each other, a sense of community motivates people to want to contribute.

Before our company adopted and fully embraced this culture of openness, transparency, and shared accountability, the top-down communication from senior management to our employees did not penetrate or resonate to the extent it does today.

Prior to our use of social technology in the office, executives at Enterasys used to send out regular company-wide emails with what we perceived to be exciting and relevant news; but we would wonder if anyone was actually reading this. There was no simple opportunity for feedback, for people to ask questions, offer suggestions, or give comments. But, in today's social environment, a simple "like" on a post gives us a sense of connection and reach. Today, a social message from our CEO allows people to easily click "I like this," and he knows right away if the message is received and understood. It is very common for our employees to comment on posts, which creates a sense of community. When there's a sense of community, people want to help the company succeed. This interactive communication method breaks down barriers. Employees feel accountable to their peers and readily willing to help build cross-functional relationships. Ultimately, the business moves faster because we have implemented community-creating social media tools in our office.

Humanizing the Business

Humanizing the business by personalizing communication with employees, especially from the top down, doesn't happen overnight. We weren't always a social business, comfortable having informal communication with the upper echelon of the company. The first time our CEO attempted to "chat" was while he was filling his gas tank at a local convenience store. The 7-Eleven was having a 'Slurpee special': fill up your gas tank and get a tall Slurpee free. Thinking other employees might appreciate a free tasty treat with a fill-up he took out his mobile phone and posted to chatter: "Free Slurpee at this gas station." Immediately, calls went to IT by employees who assumed the CEO's account had been hacked. A thousand employees never thought that Chris would ever chat about Slurpees to the entire company. IT instantly mobilized to look into it. They called Chris to warn him, and he said, "I just typed that!" This all happened within minutes, and remains one of our funniest stories about being a social company.

You see, an integral part of social adoption is to have fun with it. Work is hard; competing and winning in today's market is challenging and tough. Employees work to make a difference, and it is easy to lose sight of the fact that unless you are having fun, it is impossible to maintain momentum. But when the CEO decides to embrace social collaboration, and have fun with it, it reminds the entire company that we are all people, working for people, serving people, being human. So, get the job done, but have fun with it too.

Don't Do Social; Be S.O.C.I.A.L.

The best advice we can give you as you embark on adopting a social mindset is not to do social, but rather to be social. Being social consists of a set of attributes that helps people connect and build relationships. We use an acronym to help remind us of these attributes: Sincere. Open. Collaborative. Interested. Authentic. Likeable.

It takes practice to be social. It also takes a different kind of communication medium to highlight and capture the social attributes of a person, group, or company. It's hard to be consistently sincere, open, collaborative, interested, authentic, and likeable through email. But in the short, contextual way that social media provides you can do just that and have fun with it.

Part of the purpose of momentum and growth in a business is to celebrate the small victories along the way. In the quality world, we talk about the Kaizen approach, developed by the Japanese, which dictates that small, continuous, incremental improvements over time make a big difference. Someone might look back after two years and say: "My goodness, look what you've done! What's the one thing that transformed your business so successfully?" But from your point of view, there wasn't a big bang; it was simply a series of little things that accumulated gradually in the spirit of continuous improvement. S.O.C.I.A.L. allows you to really understand this concept, and creates an ability to celebrate, promote, and share the successes that happen along the way, so that you maintain a winning attitude as a company.

To achieve sustainable growth, healthy companies are driven by the credo "purpose first, technology second." Technology has made it easier to personalize a business's culture. But it's not just about personalization because a social business is motivated by real-time information sharing, allowing for more timely and informed decisions. Every information source in a social business is connected and part of your social network graph - a matrix of interrelated sources that provide content that can be leveraged to produce knowledge and better understanding.

In a modern business, the information sources don't just point to people. Today, machines are also connected to your network, producing relevant information for people to consume.

A true social enterprise consists of social people, social machines, and products. Any information in your ecosystem should be part of your social grasp, because ultimately, you want to be able to make informed decisions as things happen in your organization, and you want to be able to capture them in a timely and consumable manner.

Getting back to the dubious concept of the "underdog mentality"— as a scrappy company, you have a choice to either roll with what's been handed to you, or to fight your way out of it. It's ultimately your choice whether you're ready and willing to embark on this social journey.

We often talk to companies bigger than our own about social business and a how to establish a culture of collaboration, transparency, and co-creation. Any time we talk about social collaboration, the first thing that the big companies say is, "Well that's great for your small company, but for our company, it wouldn't work." Inside, we think, "That's bullshit!" but we smile politely and attempt to explain that caring for each other and being interested in one another is not a scale issue.

Excuses are bricks used to build a house of failure. Too often, big businesses are building cities of failure by not appreciating the fact that people work for people. Along the same lines, people will leave or stay because of people. In order to build a vibrant culture, you have to ignore size and focus on what matters: connecting purposefully to achieve a common goal, delighting your employees and customers, and building something that lasts. We admire big companies like IBM, SAP, Intel, Dell, and Salesforce.com that are building vibrant social communities with employees numbering in the tens of thousands.

Let us not forget: a social business is still a business, and this means it still needs governance and the measures of traditional success. All of the traditional business metrics like revenue, margins, profit, customer retention—everything that conservative 100-year-old brick-and-mortar businesses use to measure—are the ones we use too. There are no magic formulas for success specific to a social business. It's simply about how you approach solving problems.

We believe that there are more smart people outside of our company than inside our company. This is true for any business, regardless of size and market dominance. For this reason, open-minded companies that are willing to collaborate on the outside will ultimately achieve long-term sustainability and growth. But if you can learn to collaborate well internally, you will always have an advantage.

Your inside customers are just as important as your outside customers. In fact, if you can't serve your inside customers well, you will never be able to delight your external customers. Tom Peters said, "If you want to wow your customers, wow the people who are responsible for wowing your customers." We don't buy that any of these principles are good for only small businesses. For large businesses, it simply takes a larger community of smarter, socially-committed people, but the blueprint is the same.

In 2012, our company received numerous product quality, social technology innovation, and customer service industry awards. Recently, we were presented with a "Manufacturing Leadership 100" award at a conference attended by some of the largest companies in the world. All the attendees at the conference were interested in why we won the awards, but more importantly, they were interested in the fundamentals of our business process. Our response was simple: our business growth has been fueled by a transformation that prioritized critical success factors starting with culture, people, process, and technology. Most of the conference attendees were keenly aware of these pillars, and yet they wanted to know exactly how we did it.

When you are small company, and you are not competing based on brand recognition and market awareness, you are forced to adopt a focused discipline that leverages both internal and external forces to build momentum. For us, the momentum was word-of-mouth marketing. We recognized early on that each employee, customer, and business partner must be an advocate of our company. To achieve such advocacy, we knew we must first establish trust and gain loyalty. What is loyalty? If your customer continues to purchase from you and is willing to stand up for you and speak favorably of your work, then you have a loyal customer.

A social business is open and inclusive. Part of the "winning underdog" mentality means being able to adopt a pragmatically optimistic view of your business, customers, and partners. As the smaller player fighting the giants of your industry, you are forced to make good, timely decisions or you risk losing.

One successful decision we made at Enterasys was to embrace social collaboration to better improve business agility and the collective network of our employees and customers. This was clearly a choice to pivot around a concept that linked together our lines of business (marketing, sales, services, engineering, and finance) like never before. We started to develop communities, focused on a variety of business-driver initiatives, and collaborated beyond the traditional senior management circles. The results were remarkable. While we admit that it may be harder to make these kinds of changes in a bigger business, we know it can be done. At the end of the day, the challenges that face any business are mostly unrelated to size. The core values and guiding principles that served as our compass to growth and success are the same principles that can be applied to a business of any size.

Underdogs win because they know they can, but even confident underdogs must find ways to sustain momentum. A winning team is motivated by team success. A winning team is also encouraged by individual accomplishments. Social collaboration is making sure that all positive accomplishments, at any level, are acknowledged and celebrated.

Technology is Making Us Feel More Connected, Not Less

We hear so much these days about how technology is depersonalizing our culture, but in this book we demonstrate how to create greater personalization, and incorporate more human interaction into business culture. There's no question that when you have at your disposal a tremendous amount of new technologies you can get distracted. "Shiny object syndrome" can defocus an organization that is too eager to get behind a new technology before they define a lean process and come up with a commonly understood purpose.

There are a lot of tools out there, and each technology vendor is touting their solution as the one that can put your company at the top. So what should business executives think about as they embark on a social transformation? They certainly cannot ignore technology. The fastest way to lose market share and become irrelevant is to be caught on the wrong side of the digital divide. On the wrong side, management still believes that mobile, social, cloud, big data, and modern enterprise are technology fads, when in actuality they are major lifestyle shifts that offer companies the opportunity to become more strategy-driven.

Every business has to be able to utilize the most modern and the most effective tools, even if those tools change quickly. A sign of true business intelligence is the ability to adapt to change in a pragmatic and timely manner. At our company, we always keep an open mind when it comes to emerging technologies. We are curious, adaptive, free of prejudice, and able to stay ahead of the steady-state adoption curve. Historically, we have made it a priority to adopt new technologies quickly if, and only if, the technology helps us to improve execution velocity and our effectiveness when it comes to serving our customers.

As you read about our company's adoption of technology, you might be thinking that a high tech company would naturally be more inclined and more comfortable with use of new solutions, including social collaboration tools. It must be in our DNA, right? As a 30-year-old technology company, we remember the communication methods of fax, phone, email, intranets, and instant messaging. Over time, each medium offered a more seamless method of exchanging information than the one before it. Yet, there is something vastly different about today's social technology. Now, our employees are mobile and social outside of our business, and many are using tools that are far more powerful than most businesses are able, or willing, to offer. You see, for most people who are on Twitter and Facebook, who use smartphones, and tablets, communication via social networks is a lifestyle. So what if your company's DNA is lacking the technology adoption strand? In this social era, if you are unable to provide the same or better tools than your employees and customers are using at home, then you are at a talent acquisition and retention disadvantage.

Efficiency gain is one of the many benefits yielded by strategic use of social collaboration. Many companies prioritize efficiency gain ahead of effectiveness, but there is more to collaboration than just increasing speed. In some cases, companies look to over-automate to even further achieve efficiency gains; this should be avoided. The real benefit of collaboration is not just timely exchange of information, but the potential for real connections. Real connections are the ones that matter to both parties. It's these connections that are able to withstand the test of time because they are established based upon mutual trust and respect.

We see people trying to outsmart technology, those who get "clever" by automating their feeds. But if you can't do something well manually, if you can't build relationships and connect to people truthfully, please don't try to automate it. Automating system collaboration will only exacerbate social flaws or the inability to make lasting social connections. The reason why Twitter and Facebook and other social media platforms become less personalized is because people try to take shortcuts, they create automated streams that post at scheduled times. But there are no shortcuts to building lasting relationships. At Enterasys, there are real people on the other end of our Twitter and Chatter accounts, real people answering questions and comments in real time. It is important to be able to filter the right content, communicate what is relevant, and establish meaningful connections. The signal-to-noise ratio is something to be mindful of; try not to create more noise with the promise of finding more followers simply because you are active. Instead, the goal of social collaboration should be to teach and to be taught. When you exploit technology by automating it to the point where it loses its passion and focus, that's when it will overwhelm you and stop serving you. That is what has already happened to us with email.

Today, the millennial generation is hyper-connected, mobile, and maintain near constant connectivity to their friends via text message, chat, and social media forums. Sometimes, it seems like they are ignoring what's happening around them in "real life." But if you look beyond this first impression, the truth is that through technology, they have embraced a new level of connectivity that was not possible ten years ago.

Many of us have had the experience of using Facebook to reconnect with people we haven't seen in decades. Now, from across the country or across the world, we get to feel connected to them, we are privy to glimpses of how they are living their lives. We see that they took their kids to Disney World last week and had a great time. Then, if we happen to run into them on the street, we feel more intimately connected to them, despite not having actually seen them in years. This is, without question, a pervasive element of social media: consistent connection and intimacy. The same principles apply to business; an evolved level of intimate connection and trust can be formed through social collaboration.

This new paradigm rubs against the convictions of people who are used to face-to-face interactions, or those who are used to being on the phone, and many don't necessarily like typing with their thumbs or having to be eloquent within the confines 140 characters. But the fact is, it's a connection—a personal social connection. When done right, social media is not distracting, it's enabling, and without question these technological intimacies provide bridges that we did not have before.

A Culture of Trust Breeds Value

If you have an open, trusting company culture, you can recognize the highest benefit from social technologies. In an open, collaborative and safe environment employees will leverage innovation effectively, quickly, and with purpose. Something we often hear from big businesses is, "How do I control what my employees are going to say in the social stream?" The fact is, if you have to worry about what your employees are going to say, you have areas for improvement in your company's culture. It's the company's responsibility to create a culture wherein their employees won't want to complain, instead collaborate together to find ways to improve. Hiring for attitude and training for aptitude will ensure your employees are a good cultural match. Hire the people you trust, and then trust them to do the work. An advantage of a social business is that you can trust and validate because the transparencies that exist between the employees and management foster a trust-based environment.

Trust, a combination of competence and intention, has to be earned. In our sales department, when a salesperson alters their sales forecast, we have alerts and escalation rules that let the entire community know about our progress. Forecast changes are broadly communicated even to departments beyond the sales organization. This is the same sort of accountability that is promoted in professional sports. We'll talk more about "gamification" later on, but think of the analogy of an athlete in an arena. Because the scoreboard is so obvious and public, everyone knows how that athlete is doing whether she is winning or losing, and whether she is an asset or a liability to her team at any given moment. The score is the score, it's non-negotiable, and a company-wide showing ensures accountability.

In business, you also have an audience. There are players, coaches, and competition; the arena is just as vibrant, and the stakes just as important. In business, the scoreboard can't just show the final score—whether a sales opportunity was won or lost, for example. The scoreboard must also showcase performance throughout the game; it must display all of the elements of the game long before the final buzzer is heard. The scoreboard displays whether each team player is helping the business win or lose, whether they're getting penalties or rebounds or points. Professional athletes are driven to win by their very nature. Still, without a scoreboard, it wouldn't matter.

When you have an ethos that nothing is more important than your customers, you establish advocacy, and you empower your employees to be aligned with your business objectives. Ideally, your business objectives align with your customer's needs; when your customers have their needs met they feel empowered. In the social era, customer's voices and choices are scaled and amplified. The only way the voice of the business can scale is through empowered employees and customers. Social collaboration gives your business a voice by enabling every employee of your business to represent your brand. With powerful implementation of social media, we motivate people to form communities around a common purpose. The aim is to facilitate mass collaboration and momentum.

As a social business, a highly collaborative environment with transparency acts as our scoreboard. Each "athlete" who suits up and gets in the game knows that everyone is watching, expecting them to help the team win.

Twitter Takeaways

Authenticity is the intersection of what we believe, what we say, and what we do.

A social business communicates their beliefs and the 'why' for clarity of purpose.

Effective and purposeful communication in business is the driving catalyst behind social collaboration.

A social business relies on the collaboration of employees, executives, partners, and customers.

A social business consistently offers quality products, quality service, and world-class innovation.

Delighting our internal customers is the first step towards successfully delighting our paying, external customers.

Employees and customers look for authentic engagements that only a social business can deliver.

The pursuit of social business excellence is the pursuit of effective mass collaboration and shared accountability.

Social collaboration is a mindset that unlocks the full potential of an organization.

A social business has the ultimate goal of business: agility, and employee and customer delight.

A social business uses accountability and measured results across functional boundaries to maintain forward momentum.

Discipline, transparency, and reliability drive the culture of accountability in a social business.

In a social business, organizations talk about learning from their mistakes and consistently share the good, the bad and the ugly.

A social business has a purpose that's meaningful and relevant to their market, customers, and employees.

In a social business, thinkers that do rise to the top.

Our company culture is the collective personality of our employees.

A social business invests in their employees because the employee is the brand.

A social business has a flat hierarchy, ultra-clear transparency, and few boundaries between organizations.

In a social business, leaders lead without a title and ideas effortlessly reach the very top.

In a social business, momentum can be generated by an individual, but it is sustained by the community.

CHAPTER TWO:

The Social Business Mindset

"Know your business and industry better than anyone else in the world. Love what you do or don't do it." - @mcuban

The Social Business Mindset

A social business is a collaborative business which utilizes technology, culture, people, process, and strategy to achieve market-leading business results. A social business leverages the genius of the crowd—employees, customers, and business partners—to maximize its ability to adapt in the competitive, high-speed, dynamic environment of today's market. All companies face unique challenges in their particular markets as they work hard to deliver their unique products and services differentiation. Companies need to ask themselves this fundamental question: "What is different and better about our products and services that favorably sets us apart from the competition?" The answer to this question, validated by your customers, is the definition of your company's differentiation. Some companies can leverage a strong brand to achieve growth but social networking is democratizing the ability for smaller, lesser-known companies to scale their voice and value added differentiation message.

Our company is nearly 30 years old with 1,000 employees, but our brand is lesser known in wider markets. For us, one of our major challenges is that we don't have a "large" brand despite being a successful, award-winning, global company. Selling to global enterprises, our marketing focus has not been on super-bowl advertisements, or trying to become a household name. Our focus has been delivering the "best in class" technology and services to our global customers, and using our marketing dollars very judiciously to drive new sales. Because we possess a lean start-up mentality, every dollar in our business has traditionally gone back into R&D, product quality, and service quality.

When you have small market share and a lesser known brand, your business needs to rely on word-of-mouth marketing and customer advocacy in order to compete, win, and grow. For many companies, their goal is customer satisfaction. Nevertheless, over the years, we have occasionally seen satisfied customers move their business to one of our competitors. Customer satisfaction is not enough to ensure customer retention; what you really need, as a small and lean company, is customer loyalty and commitment. In order to make your products and your company sticky (or harder to detach from) with customers, you must consistently offer quality products, quality service, and world-class innovation. We have always reinvested our capital toward ensuring these three key principles are supported throughout the entire organization:

1.   Product quality: design for 10 year life-cycle with world-class reliability field quality metrics, best industry warrantees

2.   Service quality: net promoter score of 81 with global customer satisfaction of 95%

3.   Innovation: award winning portfolio of wired and wireless enterprise networking solutions

With a limited marketing budget, we continuously ask ourselves how we can increase awareness and scale our business. We realize that unless we can deliver to our internal customers, we can't deliver to our external customers. Our challenge has been to embrace a social collaboration mindset and adapt the technology and processes needed to increase awareness of our brand.

When we first decided to become a social enterprise, we were tasked with converting 1,000 employees into 1,000 advocates. If someone runs into an Enterasys employee at a dinner party or a baseball game and asks them casually about their job, we want them to speak from a place of pride and accomplishment. As our employees engage with partners and customers, their enthusiasm should be (and is) palpable. We want to give all our employees—and not just the salespeople—the power to expand and positively influence our customer relationships.

Recently, we spent a day at our Executive Briefing Center with executives from one of the largest law firms in the world. They are a big customer of ours, and this was an opportunity for our sales organization to bring them into our headquarters and introduce them to our own executives. However, they seemed more excited to meet with the everyday people that work behind the scenes at our company, like the folks in our service, quality, and engineering organizations. When they met the senior management team, they shook our hands and gave us pleasant smiles, but when they met the dedicated and passionate employees in our various departments, they were practically hugging and high-fiving. These personal relationships create trust. Establishing the seeds of trust through personal engagement and commitment is the key to building lifelong customer loyalty.

A social business model allows you to expand your reach so that customers and prospects can see the army of committed company employees that are working hard to deliver the right product, the right solution, and the right service for your business. One aspect of an expanded reach is to make that reach visible to your internal stakeholders, customers, and partners. Our company has always had a heritage of strong service and support capabilities as well as strong product quality, but our challenge has been how to sustain this level of exceptional quality. Becoming a social business has given us an opportunity to be more nimble, and to make corrections earlier in product and service life cycles. When you leverage social collaboration technology, you develop markers that quickly demonstrate when you're drifting away from internal and external service level agreements. Efficient and effective actions for these markers are what prevent cultural drift. It's about integrating technology into your customer relationship management processes, and not letting the technology take over.

Recently, our product quality team invested in tools that give us greater visibility into the manufacturing of our products. This enables us to shift out of crisis management mode and into preventative mode: dealing with things before they become fires. The faster you go the more of an opportunity you have to fall down, hard. So you need to make sure that you have the discipline and the training to sustain velocity, to course-correct and adjust as needed in real time. A social business cannot afford to be stagnant and in reactionary mode, instead it must adopt an offensive mindset. In a hyperconnected and mobile world, our ability to connect in a meaningful way is only achieved with a relentless pursuit of relevant and contextual data.

The Elements of Trust

Harvard Business Review recently published a blog by David Armano (@armano) called "On Social Media Becoming Social Business." In his post, Armano highlights how social technologies can be utilized to help define and build a social business. He defined "social business" as a purposeful, planned, orchestrated, integrated way of doing business in a social context, in order to make personal connections and to engage with the outside world. Customers look for authentic interactions, they want to feel like they are connected and have a level of authenticity when engaging with their suppliers. Any business strives to engage in this way because it's how trust is built with customers, and trust builds customer loyalty.

Within Enterasys, we have established a system to connect our global factories to our global customer base all within a "single-pane of glass," in a cloud-enabled data application, which provides authentic and proactive engagement with our customers. This is one of the ways we build trusting relationships with both our customers and our vendors. Having a social business with transparency and accessibility is what provides bottom-line results and yields lifetime customers. This synergistic model allows us to maximize the total lifetime value of our customers by achieving the best possible customer retention, year after year. This, however, is not a math success story, driven by retention percentages and lifetime value equations. This is a mission of converting our customers into loyal advocates, and we believe a social collaboration mindset is exactly the winning approach that enables us to accomplish this mission.

There are two elements to trust: there's the element of competence, and there's the element of intention. If you can demonstrate competence and intention simultaneously, you are in good shape. We often say "Fix the customer first, then the problem." When a customer contacts us with an issue, we want to make sure we give them our undivided attention, show them diligence, listen to them carefully, and demonstrate our intentions. Owning their problem, until we achieve full resolution in a timely and effective manner is how we demonstrate our intentions. In other words: "Dear customer, it's our problem until it is no longer yours."

Our customers don't have homogenous Enterasys networks because our solutions portfolio doesn't offer every single point product that a customer needs in order to run a network. Initially, we may not know if a customer's problem is with our equipment or with another vendor that is part of their network. Never-the-less, the golden rule is this: never point fingers. Part of "fixing the customer before fixing the problem" means that we take accountability for the problem, no matter what. Remember the mantra again: "It's our problem until it's no longer yours." Many of our customers point to this attitude as a particular point of pleasure in their dealings with our company. As Gary Vaynerchuck (@garyvee) noted in his book, "The Thank You Economy," the best marketing strategy is to care more. At Enterasys, that's exactly how we compete and win.

We fundamentally believe that a social business consists of people that are bound by common beliefs, which drive them to care more. Here's the thing, it costs us more to be a social business in the short run, but in the long run there's a payoff with the total value of each lifetime customer. Nothing is free; sharing valuable content consistently, and being fully engaged by listening, learning, and sharing takes time and energy. If you did a regression analysis and looked at the spending history of some of our customers, you might say that their business hasn't justified our going the extra mile... not yet, anyway. But we believe that thinking in the long-term and being patient are the hallmarks of a successful social business. We don't let short-term inconveniences get in the way of long-term benefits. Ultimately, we build lasting customer relationships by caring more than our competitors.

Our company is generating products and services in a multibillion-dollar market. Giants dominate the market of today, and every time we win we are successfully facing and beating these giants. With that said, we have less than 2% of this market. One could naively argue that when you represent only 2% of the market share, advocacy is not important because 98% of the networks out there are not ours. So how do we compete knowing our size is not an advantage? Well it turns out our size is an advantage. We are the perfect size company to do business with. How do you define a perfect size company? Quite simply, a perfect size company is one that consistently delivers on its promises.

Our biggest weapon is always "caring more." You can't be a successful social business if you don't demonstrate that you care more than your competitors. A connected consumer is smart and able to detect business authenticity with the first interaction. There's no secret ingredient, no shortcut. If you want to create customer advocacy, simply exceed customer expectations. Meeting customer expectations does not move the advocacy needle, but in today's market being consistently above average can exceed some of our customer's expectations. Of course, we don't aim for being just above average. As John Wooden said, "Being average means you are as close to the bottom as you are to the top." Average is over in the social era; we have to aim higher to compete and win.

An example of aiming higher in customer support can be found in our sourcing strategy. Most call centers in the market that we compete against have been outsourced, but when you outsource your customer service, you are outsourcing to a provider that is not motivated have the same incentive you have to build connections and relationships with your customers. In a space such as ours, we have to rely on word–of-mouth to compete and win, so we manage our own internal call center. As a social business, we value the customer relationship, the partner relationship and the employee relationship equally. Our company is only as good as the company we keep; fortunately for us, we have kept the very best, and the results are profound.

Social businesses retain great employees, develop a sense of community and nurture teamwork that is focused on a common goal. Enterasys was recently voted the one of the best places to work in Boston by "Boston Business Journal." Since 2005, our customer service and support contact centers have experienced less than 2 % annual employee attrition, as compared to industry attrition levels of 20% and higher. The average company tenure of our service and support professionals is over twelve years, and our engineering talent and service professionals have ample opportunity to go work elsewhere - Boston is one of the major engineering hubs in the country. Even as executives, we get contacted by recruiters on a weekly basis. But we all stay true to our company, and that speaks to our winning attitude, and to our culture of recognizing our employees. We are all involved, and we are proud to watch our business thrive and grow. Our loyalty to our business is directly reflected in the loyalty we earn from our customers.

Eliminating Surprises

"It's not knowing what to do, it's doing what you know." - @tonyrobbins

When a customer contacts a representative in one of our support centers, a ticket opens in our call center, and because of our social mindset, a sales associate and a solutions engineer are both automatically notified by our system. In a technology company, a customer ordinarily deals with a solutions engineer and an account executive. If a customer calls us from South Dakota with an issue, our system automatically identifies the account executive and the solutions engineer for that geographic region. As soon as the case is opened, the system emails those individuals to alert them about the customer's case. In a social business you want to eliminate any surprises. The worst case scenario would be if one of our sales colleagues tried to pitch a new solution to a client an hour after that client experienced a network outage. We eliminate the potential for these awkward errors with our use of automated social technology. Real-time context is delivered to the sales colleague immediately so that she walks into every meeting and makes every phone call completely informed.

Data Driven – Good; Knowledge Driven – Better; Action Driven – Best

We keep using the words "collaboration" and "transparency," but what does all this mean, and are the two words interrelated? Any one of us responsible for managing a business in any capacity is always looking for data that's insightful enough to help us make better, more informed decisions. At the end of the day, no matter what level you are at in your organization, whether you're a sales contributor or a CEO, you're asked to make a lot of decisions every minute, every hour, every day. Data doesn't necessarily equate to knowledge, and knowledge doesn't necessarily equate to actionable understanding. Part of what transparency is about is correlating all possible information so you can make more well-informed decisions. Every information node—and we use the word "node" because we get our information from a variety of sources, including people, products, and technology—can be used to help make more informed decisions.

Our Social Machines - ISAAC

We were the first company to invent social machines. We're proud to say that nobody else has products that can communicate to humans on social networks such as Twitter, Facebook and Salesforce.com's Chatter. One of our most successful inter-company technologies is a product we invented called ISAAC. Although the inventor, Vala Afshar, had great innovators and inventors, like Isaac Newton, on his mind, he actually named the technology based on the ISAAC acronym: Intelligent Socially Aware & Automated Collaboration. The concept is simple and it takes advantage of social, mobile, cloud and consumer technology (available through smartphones and tablets) that is dominating the enterprise with a design emphasis on improving the user experience. The question we asked ourselves was why can't our social, mobile and highly connected customers securely manage and control their networks, by connecting to machines, using social media? With ISAAC they can.

ISAAC has won numerous awards since its inception, and more than half a dozen industry awards just in 2012 alone. The ISAAC technology is a social media interface that acts as a translator between the machine world and the human world. ISAAC is designed to convert complex machine language into something humans can easily understand (English, German, Spanish, Japanese), so our customers can easily manage their complex enterprise networking machines. Rather than explain exactly how ISAAC works, we'll give you a working scenario that should suffice:

Education is our strongest sales vertical market and it's where the majority of our company revenue comes from. Higher education caters to the most elite customers. The average college student checks her smart phone or tablet every ten minutes. There's a new term for this: "F.O.M.O.," Fear of Missing Out. Students tend to be so connected that if they are in a situation where they don't have the opportunity to check their devices constantly, the stress of being denied access actually becomes more of a source of distraction than the device was in the first place. This is a counter-intuitive concept, but studies have shown that if you deny students the use of their electronics, they actually have a harder time absorbing the information that's being delivered to them.

Based on our experience working with hundreds of colleges and universities, we see that today the average college student has four machines on their person most of the time: a tablet, a smart phone, a laptop, and either an e-reader or a gaming device. Studies predict that in a few years this number is going to reach six or seven with the addition of wearable IP devices, badge readers, Google glasses, sensors, and other internet protocol (IP) devices that are connected and networked.

We appreciate how all of our employees produce insightful information in an ecosystem of social collaboration, but we also have machines that produce a lot of useful information as well. The information these machines produce is vital to our business and growing in numbers. In addition to educational institutions, we serve hospitals, banks, and other mission-critical big businesses, including well-known federal and state agencies. So clearly, we have customers whose enterprises fundamentally rely on the consistent and reliable operation of our products. In order to manage mission- critical networks, you have to have visibility into, and control of, the machines. Traditionally, this sort of visibility and control didn't happen in a social construct; with ISAAC, it now does.

Let us explain. Many of our employees are under the age of thirty. Studies show that if you're under thirty, 90% of the time you spend on the internet is on social media: Facebook, Google+, Instagram, Pinterest, Yammer, Twitter, and so on. Young professionals have grown up comfortably with social media and portable personal devices; that's where they spend their time connecting with people they trust and care about. Our young, bright IT professionals are already on social media. So when something goes wrong with the network, its common sense that the fastest way to get in touch with an IT person is through the medium they're already used to communicating in. With ISAAC, we have devised a way to convert the language of our machines to human social language. The invention is a simple bi-directional interpreter of machine language to social language. We could write a few chapters, or perhaps dedicate an entire book, on ISAAC, but that would diverge from the main point. The biggest take away for our readers is that there will soon be more machines connected to the Internet than there will be humans. Projections have targeted 50 billion connected machines to the internet by 2020 as compared to human population that is projected to be 7 billion plus. This means that our social network graph will include people and products.

One-sixth of humanity is on Facebook and Twitter, and Facebook is slated to reach a billion users this year. Out of the world's 7 billion people, 1.5 billion are on at least one of these two social networks. So, when we started to design ISAAC, we focused on these two social networking platforms, along with a third: Salesforce.com's Chatter. Salesforce.com is a leading automated CRM product, and Chatter is essentially a proprietary Facebook-type tool they created for enterprise communication. Because our employees were already accustomed to using Chatter for their internal communication, it was a natural choice when we extended our conversations to include our machines.

We wanted ISAAC to be a secure technology, so we purposefully bolted the ISAAC logic on top of our network management software suite. There is one machine in the network—the network management machine—that sees all the other machines, allowing us to poll, monitor, and control all activity and interconnections on the network. This one machine captures all of the information from the entire network so that we can essentially use it as an interpreter. As traditional machine language comes into this management console, it is converted into a configured Twitter, Facebook, or Chatter interface.

We'll talk more about ISAAC in a later chapter, but for now, let's just say that the really good news is that we have patented this technology to easily port so that we can convert it into machine-to-machine language for other companies too. The language was designed in a portable fashion so it could be licensed later. The patent is currently pending and, if it is awarded to us, it will become applicable to all sorts of location-based technology. Think: thermostats and home security systems. Imagine driving home after being away from your house for a week and receiving a tweet from your home thermostat—which has figured out your location by talking to your car's GPS—to ask you if you want to turn the thermostat up or the air conditioning on. With a simple tweet back, you could easily confirm an action. You could actually talk remotely to your own house in this way. This is one of the many possibilities of a machine-originated social network.

Car manufacturers, in fact, are already integrating social collaboration into their machinery. In a few years, when you get a flat tire or your check engine light comes on, the car itself will notify the nearest tow station or car dealership. Toyota was the first to jump on the "social vehicles" bandwagon with their "Toyota Friend" service, and now Ford and all the other car companies are getting on board too. It is our belief that absolutely all machines can one day be a part of the social network and have communication channels through social media networks.

There's no way you can commit to research and development, or to do something that's first–in–industry unless you really believe in the concept of being a social company. So far, Enterasys is the only company that has built its own social machine-to-machine product.

In a July 2012 Forbes article, entitled Social Machines: How This Company is Using Artificial Intelligence to Create Social Intelligence, author Mark Fidelman said, "I've built and seen a lot of Salesforce.com implementations but nothing like this." Mark has written about social CIOs and CMOs for a long time. His validation is great, but more importantly ISAAC actually works so well for us.

You May Hate Gravity, But Gravity Doesn't Care

As we noted in the introductory part of this book, Clay Christensen, a professor at Harvard Business School, famously said, "You may hate gravity, but gravity does not care." As far as we're concerned, social = gravity and social is driving mobility and the greater adoption of consumer technology in the enterprise. Email and texting were just the beginning. Generation Y, and younger folks, are used to being connected all the time; they write short, personalized messages to communicate with their friends and followers in the moment. The social mobile revolution is not about technology; it's about a lifestyle. Any CEO, CIO, or CXO who thinks that mobility and social are irrelevant is simply fighting gravity. We're nowhere near the tipping point in terms of social activity, let alone social products, so somebody who's just hearing about social machines like ISAAC probably thinks it is pulled from the pages of Science Fiction.

As you read this, universities are connecting to Enterasys via social networks. The universities are connecting their IT staff and their machines via Salesforce.com's public social network called Chatter. The best part of this is that their machines are communicating to our machines and doing most of the manual work that our customers would traditionally have to do for themselves. The machines are also performing the customer service work that our engineers would normally transact manually. Yes, machine to machine social collaboration with automated services delivery.

Machine communication is coming into our business and being converted to actionable work that engages our employees. A machine at a customer network lets us know if something is wrong; we automatically create a ticket based on that communication, and before the customer even knows there's a problem, we are working on a resolution and communicating details back to them. The entire service lifecycle is machine-to-machine via a social network. It truly is an industry first.

The beauty of all of this isn't that the machines are talking by social; it's that a customer, instead of spending time troubleshooting and manually contacting us to remedy a given situation, is doing more important things and letting the machine solve the problem in the background. It is not necessary to have as many people operating the phones, doing the diagnostics and the administrative work, because the CRM system is doing it for us. Only if an issue becomes really complicated does a human need to get involved. As far as trivial issues are concerned, the services lifecycle is faster and requires zero human intervention, which makes for an incredibly efficient system. For a CEO, one takeaway might be that not only does social collaboration improve execution velocity in a business, but it also brings a scale of economy and efficiency, which cannot be replicated by simply increasing staffing levels.

One critical metric that all CEOs and CIOs utilize in regard to their network is "uptime." They rely on their network being up and running as much as possible. To a business, a network is as important as the roof on the building. If it goes down, business stops. Network uptime is therefore of critical interest to any CIO or CEO, and ISAAC helps maximize network uptime. It takes proactive problem solving into the world of automation, and if it's used right, it can be massively effective.

As of the time we are writing this book, we've won half a dozen industry innovation awards and have been interviewed a dozen times by Forbes, Information Week, ZDNet, and other publications about ISAAC.

Customer Perception is Our Reality to Manage

In order for non-market leading companies   to compete and win, they must   leverage   the   strength   of every individual   on   the team. Better yet, smaller companies must leverage the strength of the entire ecosystem, which consists of employees, customers and partners to bolster their scale and ability to compete. In order to have internal advocacy—meaning that the sales organization trusts the services organization, the services organization trusts the engineering organization, etcetera—each has to have demonstrated value to the others.

An example of delivering internal value added services in our company is the linkage between sales and services. At Enterasys, the services organization produces social dashboards in our CRM tool so that we can create a linkage between forecasted sales opportunities and potentially open tickets in our call centers. We filter important, high-dollar-amount sales opportunities so that sales colleagues never complain that they lost a potential deal because of poor service quality. It's crucial that our services organization has visibility into sales for this reason.

Because we have established services visibility into sales opportunities, we need an intelligent approach to make sure we keep an eye on the opportunities that matter, so we have created a dollar amount threshold (something like $50,000 and above) and a report of any opportunities that fall above this threshold. We call such opportunities "Hot Deals." Within a given "Hot Deals" population, we filter out how many of these are existing customers with open support cases. If a customer has a support case open, there is a possibility for dissatisfaction, so we filter those cases into another column called "Hot Accounts."

Typically, out of one hundred customers in a "Hot Deal" population, you may find less than ten customers that have open cases. These ten represent "Hot Account" opportunities. Because our business is social and transparent, we've created automated dashboards that show all of our Hot Deals and Hot Accounts and automatically push this information to the sales organization. At any time, any member of our sales department can log on to this dashboard through our sales CRM and see the current stats. We've further subdivided it into global dashboards, regional dashboards, and account-executive dashboards.

Our sales organization considers their access to service data to be a major value-added service into their business. It helps them do their jobs more effectively, and it helps eliminate any problem that could derail a client relationship. After all, you can have all the metrics in the world, and you can beat your chest over all the bugs you've found, but it only takes one unmanaged problem at a customer's site to find yourself instantly replaced by another vendor.

Customer perception is our reality to manage, so we capture all of the quality trends for a given product and we push those dashboards to our engineering organization as well. Our engineers assess product quality based on customer perception, which is more important than any internal metric we keep. Because of their ability to get this detailed information so easily, engineering now views services as a value-added partner and a trusted advisor to help them get their job done. Collaboration in a social business provides a high degree of visibility that leads to shared accountability and strong levels of advocacy.

Living in the Cloud

Most CEOs will read this far and probably agree that it sounds like a fundamentally good idea for any business to be a social business. But it's one thing to speak to it and another thing entirely to do it. It's inarguably a good idea to share performance metrics across lines of business, and it's great to be proactive, but are you willing to spend seven figures annually to do all of this? Enterasys is a small company, but we're spending over a million dollars a year on our CRM solution with Salesforce.com. To be able to deliver real-time performance reporting through dashboards, and insight from one line of business to another requires a real financial investment.

Today at Enterasys a customer can log on to our CRM self-service portal and submit a case to us through the web. More importantly, they can view their open cases. They can also access a 12-month summary report right from the dashboard. We capture, log, and collate all of the information we get from them, the products they call about, how they contacted us (phone, email, and dashboard), whether they experienced a defect in the software or hardware, and who called it in. All of this information is captured and displayed so the customer has as much visibility regarding their case as we do. Effectively, it's like they're inside our kitchen watching us cook the meal. It is a signature of a social business to have complete collaboration, and to adopt complete transparency.

We use a fusion of all of the core technology trends that are shaping today's IT landscape—mobility, cloud, big data, social—through tools like ISAAC and the other technologies that we enable through our business. Every one of our customers gets to see behind the curtain. We show our customers and partners exactly why we make the decisions we make, and we show them the data we collect about them as a customer, even if it's sensitive data. We show our customers everything from detailed factory data output to software test plans. At Enterasys we rely on tools that are cutting edge technology, which enables our business to be transparent, nimble and accountable.

Universal ideas of transparency and openness apply to all businesses. Today's economy is a global economy; as a United States based company, we have to compete with much different marginal labor rates across the globe. We compete with larger companies that have more resources, and smaller companies that can be quicker and lighter on their feet. We see a full spectrum of competition. Being a social business allows us to provide a personal connection and collaborate across boundaries and throughout organizations. This is not an idea that's specific to any one size business, it's universal.

We rely on our social tools to give us the data we need, in the right context, at the right time. ISAAC helps give our customers maximum network uptime, and in this way, we service them at a higher level. In the information sharing economy it is more than just the right content at the right time: it is about context, which enables efficiency for all stakeholders. It is a value exchange ethos, as opposed to a value extraction with execution velocity and intimacy at the core of each touch point. Our ability to be available, responsive and informed is how we transform each transaction into an engagement opportunity.

Here's the takeaway: if you're not sharing company and departmental performance metrics with your customers and partners, you're not a social business. If you don't have machines as part of your social network graph, you're not a social business. You can debate this philosophy left and right, but it's what we're doing at Enterasys, and it's working. We are continually growing, outpacing the market, and winning awards. Being a social business is what gives us our winning edge.

Twitter Takeaways

A perfect size company is one that consistently delivers on their promises. Growth depends on reliability.

A social business is still a business. Innovation, product and service quality still matters, regardless of open mindset.

We cannot automate relationship building. A shift from transactions to engagement is not about automation.

Fix the customer first, and then fix the problem. "Dear customer, it's our problem until it's no longer yours."

A social business is farsighted and patient. Go fast, look far, but don't hurry.

Avoid outsourcing your core competencies. Ask yourself, what do we do best? Then do that, yourself.

A social business loves their employees, customers and partners. Yes, loves.

A social business is understanding and action driven. Data sharing must lead to action to matter.

In the social era, we must listen loudly, engage kindly and deliver value enthusiastically.

In the social era, both people and products must be part of the social network graph.

In the social era, understanding our customer's customer need is how we become trusted advisor.

Ask your customer: "who is your favorite company to do business with and why?" then listen and learn. A win-win question.

A customer's perception is your reality to manage. Never assume customer delight.

Customer feedback is a gift. Accept graciously, unwrap enthusiastically and share with your team.

In a social business, departmental performance metrics are shared across the lines of business.

In a social business, a dynamic and vibrant communication is achieved based on mutual trust and respect.

Big ego, small ears. In a social business mostly everyone has very, very big ears.

Integration of social channels into your CRM is the only way to optimize social collaboration.

In a social business, executive management is actively using CRM tools to collaborate. Leadership is example.

A social business leverages communication to flatten its company hierarchy – best ideas win, not the best titles.

CHAPTER THREE:

Laying the Groundwork for Social Business Excellence

The groundwork for social business excellence contains six crucial elements. The order of these business elements pertains directly to the impact they will have on your social business transformation.

1.   Culture – the collective personality of your business is your culture. The core values and guiding principles of your business will have the biggest impact on your ability to transform your company into a social business.

2.   People – hire the people you trust, and trust them to their work. As we look at our company's continued success, it is without a doubt due to the people who shape our future. It is true the best players usually win, but it is not about how smart you are, or your past accomplishments, rather, it is how much you care about the future and the people you work with. It is the character of our people that shape our company's future.

3.   Strategy – in a social business, what you believe and why must be communicated to all levels of the organization, and it must be aligned with a shared purpose that is both meaningful and realistic. What is the best strategy? Care more.

4.   Process – a social business embraces lean processes, based on the value that is places on the user experience. Lean processes, with a TLC mindset (Think Like a Customer) are in the DNA of a social business. Never build processes around a technology. Process first, technology second.

5.   Structure – the flatter the structure the easier to hear the sounds. Ideas are sounds, and they need to be heard throughout the seams of your organizational fabric. Vibrancy is noisy; be vibrant.

6.   Technology – the more innovative the organization, the more likely that it will successfully transform into a social business. Comfort with technology is the backbone of a social business. In a social business, technology is utilized to create choices, freedom and a better lifestyle for employees, customers, and partners.

The order of these foundational elements is specific, and in this chapter we will tackle them one at a time.

Culture

Culture is the collective personality of a business. Culture is based on the shared values and beliefs that shape our behavior and actions. We believe strongly in having a culture built on transparency, accountability, empowerment, collaboration, innovation, and reliability. These are the core themes that unlock the value that social technology can bring to a modern enterprise.

About six years ago, after coming out of several flat business years, Enterasys engaged in a very specific and focused effort to define our company culture around growth. For the business to change in a positive direction, the business personality needed to be defined and managed actively. It was imperative that this culture became pervasive throughout our business. A company-wide initiative to define our culture was announced by our CEO. The executive team chose an Extended Leadership Team, made up of non-management employees to spearhead the effort.

Draft cultural attributes were assembled in a survey format, distributed to employees with the following request, "We want to redefine who we are and where we are going, and we want you to be a part of this process. We need your help to define our culture as a team." The entire company was asked to participate, and over half of the employees provided written feedback for the cultural definition initiative.

We started by defining "individual traits" and "communication traits" that we desired within our business. The first feedback from the broader employee base was that people wanted to have management traits defined as well. We believe having management and employees working off the same sheet of paper is critical to having a strong culture. So, when we aggregated our culture summary attributes and behaviors, we included a section specific to management traits. A very significant amount of debate and discussion went into every word that was selected for the final draft. Multiple large session meetings with the Extended Leadership Team, and other departments, were conducted to narrow down the cultural attribute selections.

Enterasys Cultural Theme:
"There is nothing more important than our customer."

The Enterasys Culture is:
- **Optimistic**
- **Accountable**
- **Trusting and open**
- **Engaged in calculated risk**
- **Supportive of constructive change**
- **One of few layers**
- **Promoting of cross functional team**

Definition of Culture:
A shared, learned, symbolic system of values, beliefs and attitude that shapes and influences perception and behavior.

With the definition and attributes completed, we then developed a card format for the distribution and presentation of our cultural definition. The card had two primary content pages. The first was a "Company Cultural Theme" page with specific attributes. On this first page, we also defined the word "culture" to ensure employees all had the same understanding of what we were attempting to define. On the second content page was a set of contrasting behaviors that were supportive of our cultural theme and summary. The contrasting behaviors were very important because they not only provided the behavior we wanted, but also provided the context for the opposite behavior, behavior that was to be avoided. This juxtaposition was very helpful for individual adoption. People relate to specific personal behaviors more easily than high-level abstractions.

Average or Flat Company	Innovative or Growth Company
Individual Traits	**Individual Traits**
- Not my job	- Work collaboratively
- Looking backwards	- Looking forward
- Procrastination	- Do it right, do it now
- If it ain't broke, don't fix it	- Look for meaningful ways to improve
- Process for process sake	- Efficiency and effectiveness
- Work for your boss	- Empowered to be your own boss
Communication Traits	**Communication Traits**
- Hides issues	- Spotlight issues
- Suppress mistakes	- Acknowledge and correct mistakes
- Document to cover yourself	- Document to communicate properly
- Closed-minded listening	- Open collaboration
- Hoarding knowledge	- Back yourself up
- Spread rumors	- Facts and action
Management Traits	**Management Traits**
- Do as I say, not as I do	- Lead by example
- Employee training is a drain	- Training is an asset for the company
- Decision making in a vacuum	- Soliciting views from others
- Micro-management	- Trusting empowerment
- Passing blame	- Accountability and support
- Taking credit	- Giving credit
- Keeping secrets	- Honesty and transparency

Our goal was to shift our employees' focus onto the traits on the right side of the list in order to better support our company culture. Giving our people this strong road map, along with a high-level summary of our expectations and goals, was critical to the success of this project. It was also paramount that senior management was on board, and that they also abided by this same cultural roadmap. The management we had in place at the time was a new team, and they helped the overall turnaround of the business culture by adopting a "start at the top" attitude. In fact, our expectations as a company always start at the very top, because if our management team doesn't live our culture, our employees never will.

Some of the positive traits on the right side of our culture card:

- Optimism
- Accountability
- Trusting
- Open
- Engaged in calculated risk
- Supportive of constructive change
- Nimble

We spent hours specifically choosing each and every one of those words, thinking about the way each would roll off the tongue and be interpreted in different languages. While "nimble" does not translate well, we chose it anyway because it's so important that our headquarters, based in the U.S., have that particular attribute. Together, the words on this list comprise a mentality of open, "constructive change" that promotes social collaboration.

We defined our culture, we began to live it, and then we started measuring it. We put in mechanisms such as peer-to-peer recognition, where people can recognize their peers and get a small monetary incentive if they map well to our culture card. Leadership is about setting deliberate examples, and we believe in putting our money where our mouths are. Our peer-to-peer award is an American Express gift certificate for a nominal amount of $25, but it's the gesture that matters. When you walk into the cubicles and labs of some of our employees who exemplify excellence, they have wallpapered their work spaces with peer-to-peer awards. Showcasing awards is about celebrating behaviors that are supportive, inspirational and motivational amongst peers.

We give these awards in a public fashion during our team meetings, and there are rounds of applause. When we deliver them, we read off who gave what award to whom and for which cultural attribute. We are very specific about why we give each award. When we first put this incentive program in practice, it only took a few months for people to say, "Wow, I feel a change." Even partners and customers started to agree; "Suddenly, this business seems more customer-centric. People seem happier, more engaged." This intentional shift in culture had a profound impact on our business. Because we're owned by private equity, the owners occasionally send consultants in to find out how we're doing. We've had expert HR consultants come through our offices, and they have been amazed by what we've done; they've even asked us to send them examples of our cultural transformation process.

One of the most common pieces of feedback we get about these culture cards is the specificity of the traits outlined thereon. A lot of companies attempt this kind of motivation transformation, but they make the mistake of using big words that don't really mean anything, like "synergistically." People don't relate to abstractions; they relate to specific human traits, things that they can understand in a human context. Another organization might bring in "behavioral experts" or ask their managers to define a culture card, and then try to convince the rank and file to adopt these attributes. But for us, it was a grassroots effort, and every employee had a chance to be involved. The card itself was a catalyst to get everyone talking about something; that something happened to be the core values of our company.

In order to identify these core values we created a survey. A river without boundaries is just a puddle; so we couldn't simply survey 1,000 people and create a culture card straight from the overwhelming feedback the survey produced. We needed an extended leadership team, an ELT, to help us sort through the choices. Even though participation in the first ELT was voluntary, we wanted to make sure we captured the "best of the best" change agents in our company that represented different functions. The executive team talked to the managers and directors and said, "Help us fin d the people on your teams who best identify your group and represent the mindset and the winning attitude we want in this company." Our first ELT was comprised of 20-25 select members from across our ranks, and it continues to be an ongoing program with revolving chairs. The chairs are never CEO direct reports. We purposely make sure the ELT is led by volunteers that represent the front lines of our business, comprised of individuals who feel the pulse of the company closest to where the "real" work is being done. Social businesses value the input from those on the front lines.

Ultimately, a key trait of a social business is a flat hierarchy, whether the organization is literally flat or just gives a perception of being flat. At Enterasys, our CEO has over ten direct reports, so we do have a flat organization where ideas rise organically to the top. You're not a social business if an idea from a single contributor can't get to the CEO directly. With a traditional vertical hierarchy, there are obstacles between the CEO and any given employee. This makes it challenging for the employee to effectively communicate good ideas and solutions. But at Enterasys, any employee can gain the attention of the CEO through Chatter; there's no filtering.

Our ELT group has a charter to improve the business of our company through the alignment of day-to-day employee activity, which drives our ideal corporate culture of becoming an innovative company and a customer-centric business. The ELT is a communication conduit between the employees and the leadership teams, which makes it a structural mechanism as much as it is cultural. The ELT has been critical in helping our cultural initiative move forward. It's allowed for senior management consulting to provide input and feedback on bonus plans, established anonymous feedback loops on new hire activities, developed the peer-to-peer recognition award, spurred events within the business, and generally helped build a sense of community. Most importantly, it provides a quick conduit to flatten our organization and allow ideas to flow quickly through the ranks.

People

A critical element of our ethos while developing the ELT was the guiding principle that there is nothing more important than our customers.

With that guiding principle as our North Star, the organization decided what the other core values of our business should be. On our culture card, our people chose to emphasize the traits of reliability, innovation, and customer focus as the core values of Enterasys. We purposefully chose reliability as a stand-alone word because while we need our products to function correctly, we also need our people to be reliable. When you're a small company, the best way to combat prejudice against size is simple, deliver on your promises. If you consistently deliver on your promises, customers don't care how big or small you are.

Our original culture card went out of its way to emphasize what winning looks like, but also to talk about what losing looks like. A typical culture card at another company might not include losing attributes, but we put the negative qualities on our culture card, and we encouraged our employees to call out negative behavior. We made sure that each employee in all thirty of our office locations around the globe had a culture card in their hands on the morning of its release. We defined what comprised a winning attitude as well as what contributed to a losing attitude. We then encouraged people and empowered them to call out individuals that were drifting from our culture.

As many people are aware, Bostonians share a great love of their sports teams. Being headquartered in the Greater Boston area, sports are a big deal to us.   In the last seven years Boston has won a championship in every major sport. We have unbelievable athletes—Hall of Famers and All Stars—and we see some of them get traded out of Boston because of poor attitude. Chemistry matters. We top-grade, and we will replace an employee not just because of a deficiency in aptitude, but more importantly, because of a deficiency in attitude.

Every manager, every account executive, every solutions engineer, every customer-facing employee that we hire—especially in sales and services—is invited to our headquarters to meet with our CEO and his direct reports. Executives interview every sales account executive and solutions engineer; they talk to every director candidate that's in a customer-facing function. They will sit with our CEO for thirty minutes.

This is an example of how some of our practices at a small company don't necessarily scale to a much larger company. At IBM, the CEO is not going to have the time to interview every candidate, but because we are a 1,000-person company, this is feasible. We always make sure that a candidate is interviewed by someone outside of her area of the business. We want to set a precedent up front that any new hire realizes she will be working with many different lines of business at Enterasys, regardless of her specialty or role. As a candidate, you might be considered for hire in sales, yet you can rest assured that you will be interacting with engineering, services and marketing. In a social business we think less about departments and more about collaborative processes.

Within our company we have a sales doctrine, a 19-page document that we give to every salesperson, which states that the salesperson is essentially the acting CEO of the company while in the field. If you're in the field, you shape the company brand. You're empowered to delight our customers, and when you need something from corporate headquarters, we're going to respond immediately, and we're going to be available to you.

But how do we operationalize it? How do we foster that type of thinking? Well, we created a War Room, where every week the CEO and his direct reports meet and discuss cases that have been submitted. Any customer-facing employee at any level within our sales or services organizations can submit a case to the War Room. It's sort of like being in front of the Supreme Court. If you have an issue that's time-sensitive, or you feel that something requires a decision from the highest level in the company in order to win a sale, you can submit a case to the War Room through our Salesforce.com CRM tool. Immediately, the CEO and his staff are notified. For example, a request might be: "I need a special pricing allowance," or "I need the Chief Customer Officer to get on the phone and talk to a client's new CIO," or "I have a product quality question for the engineering team." There are a number of reasons to engage the War Room, and any employee is at liberty to do so. There's a very minimal set of requirements, in fact, there are no filters or requirements for submitting to the War Room, but the expectation is that you will have a compelling reason to do so. We would never tax or penalize an employee for submitting something trivial to the War Room, but common sense dictates that when you submit a case to the CEO and his team, you're going to put some effort into presenting your case. Giving employees a direct and tangible channel of connection to the executive team ensures that the sales field knows they are acting CEOs of our company, and the ability to get quick executive decisions helps us all win.

We live by the theme that "none of us are as smart as all of us." Together, we make the right decisions for the company. That sense of transparency comes through in a structural tool like the War Room. It's a great symbolic representation of our culture of accountability and transparency. If a single contributor cannot raise a flag and have that flag be visible to the CEO and his staff, it's not a social business. The same is true for positive and proactive support. For instance, a request might read, "Dear executive, I have a new leader in my customer organization and I would love for you to contact them on the phone and introduce yourself." If this new executive is entering our customer's ranks already more familiar with our competition, that account is automatically at risk. A War Room submission could request that a handful of our executives get on a plane and go to the client to explain our capabilities, our culture, and our solution portfolio in person. Because it's a significant business expense, it's something that might go to the War Room for a decision.

In a social business, disposition in a particular inquiry is done in real time. Having a quick yes or no answer is valuable to the salesperson who's trying to compete and win in the field. If it's a "no," they can be creative and decide what other steps to take or whether to move away from that opportunity and fight the next battle. The key here is "accessibility." As a leader, if you're not accessible, you're not social. Part of being social is being accessible at the highest level, and social media dramatically enables that accessibility.

When it comes to recruiting new staff, we believe that the paper resume is archaic. Social businesses want to have social candidates be part of their ecosystem. We look for candidates with an online presence, particularly on social networks like Twitter. Twitter can be a good barometer of a candidate's accomplishments, networking capability, and a measure of their influence. All things being equal, if we have two candidates, we're inclined to invite the one who is more socially active. With this paradigm shift in the way that companies recruit candidates, we perform a hunt for talent rather than letting the talent come to us. The people we want to hire are busy doing their own stuff and changing the world. They're not on Monster.com or LinkedIn, and if they are, they're not active on those platforms. The last few high-level hires we've made were found on social media.

When we hire, we obviously try to find people who have the experience and match the job requirements, but very quickly, through the first phone screenings, we start to evaluate their cultural attributes to see if they will be a good fit. The first thing a candidate gets when she comes in for an interview is a welcome package with our culture card. We have a significant schedule of interviewees come through, a barrage of people and questions, but our primary screening point is always whether they are a good cultural fit. Will they sync with the personality of the business? This is absolutely critical. We have a profile of what a social employee needs to look like, and we absolutely make choices and decisions based upon that profile. Without a doubt, our hiring practices are mapped to match our culture.

Additionally, people go through cycles in their careers, so we go through the process of constantly evaluating our current talent and moving people out when they are no longer a fit. This is an extremely transparent process. It's open and honest, and people in the business understand what's happening. In a social business there is either an informal or formal 360 degree view of employee performance based on horizontal and vertical shared sentiment regarding judgment, experience, and influence of team members. This holistic approach of talent assessment is a natural element of mass collaboration that exists in a highly transparent company culture.

Regardless of your title – from single contributor to vice president – you are susceptible to peer and subordinate feedback, and this is a good thing. Because of our social culture and the feedback our employees can provide to us, we have multiple data points that speak to whether an employee is valuable and can influence change. When you think about the value of individual contributions to a company, experience and judgment come into play, and sometimes the judgment is not necessarily tied to the experience. If you have someone who hasn't been with the company very long, but exhibits sound judgment and critical thinking skills, they can simply connect the dots better.

Judgment, experience, and influence are three qualities we evaluate in every employee. You may have judgment, you may have experience, but if you're not influencing other people effectively, you're basically a smart jerk. We respect intelligence, but we admire compassion, humility, and inclusiveness as well. You might have the right idea, but if you rub people the wrong way, you turn them off. This is where influence comes into play, and it is why we look to social media as a key recruiting tactic. Certain companies, such as Peer Index and Klout and Cred, are actually trying to develop algorithms that measure a person's social currency. This sometimes feels a little yucky, but the reality is that Enterasys is a service organization. Similarly, on the customer side, if two customers contact our support organization about the same problem, we'll attend to the customer with the wider social reach first. It would be foolish of us not to focus on the customer with an amplified voice.

Of course, some people have influence but poor judgment. So it's important to equally weigh all three elements—judgment, experience, and influence—in the culture of a social business. The bottom line for us is to always stay committed to living our culture. On the back of all of our business cards it says, "There's nothing more important than our customer." In every conference room there's a giant poster displaying our culture card, because we want guests and visitors to know what we believe in. This is all part of our culture of transparency.

By the way, we aggressively recruit people who are already working. If you're working in our space, you're working for the competition, and the competition is always bigger. The four or five companies we compete with make up more than 90% of the market. So why would a candidate come to Enterasys? Why leave Cisco or HP or Juniper and come to work for a company with a smaller brand? When candidates come to Enterasys, the first thing they do is look at the culture card poster on our wall, they see a visual representation of our core values and guiding principles. When we ask people why they decided to leave their current position and come work for us, they generally say, "You know, when I left that interview, I noticed that every person I met in your company lived the culture I saw on that poster on your wall." When a person chooses to work for us, they know they will be treated and respected as an individual. Our strength is built upon our differences.

Strategy

We don't have a "mission," we have a North Star and it is: there is nothing more important than our customers. We think about the market as the wind: you can't control the wind, but if you follow your North Star—your core beliefs and your guiding principles—the wind will blow at your back.

There are things that are outside of your control, like macroeconomic factors, or a customer's bias toward a competitor. So at Enterasys, we focus on what we believe are our core values and guiding principles. We know that we have to intentionally be a social business.

We have to have grit, and we have to be humble to survive in a social business, because the price of transparency is the fact that the best ideas always win. Executives love to walk into a room, make a statement, and have everybody nod their head. But in a social business, we know that we have to be ready to recognize (and have the community recognize) the best idea—no matter who it comes from. If an executive comes up with an idea, and it gets challenged by a better idea from a subordinate, the better idea cannot be ignored, because the community is right there to remind us: "I don't understand why you ignored Beth's advice. She makes an excellent point."

Our vision—to be the best network infrastructure and security solutions company—always comes back to expanding our customer relationships beyond sales. With a limited marketing budget, we have managed to become an award-winning, highly successful company largely because of the way in which we relate to our customers.

Some of the ways we have done this include:

- Sustaining exceptional customer service, no matter what
- Creating a culture of internal advocacy
- Fully utilizing all resources at our disposal
- Bringing headquarters closer to our customers
- Lateral sharing of the best practices
- Humanizing the enterprise

Let's speak in particular to that last bullet point: humanizing the enterprise. What does this mean? To us, it means that a good business is always personal and transparent, and that accountability and trust both within our organization, and with our external customers, is pivotal. We "communicate at the speed of need." Adopting Chatter as an integrated CRM collaboration solution was one of the ways in which we humanized Enterasys. We started using Chatter in January of 2010, and in the two and a half years since, it has become a major part of the way our company communicates. Chatter allows us to bring together groups of people who are interested in relevant content, it gives all of our staff access to the executives, and keep in touch through mobile devices both on and offsite. Most importantly, our social innovation practices have made it easier for us to reward high achievers in a public way, and enabled us to create successful group practices that can be (and have been) easily adopted throughout the company. Humanizing our enterprise—and our machines, with ISAAC— has been a fundamental part of our strategy.

Process

We already talked about one of our main processes, the War Room. Another process we use at Enterasys is TLC: Think Like a Customer. This critical way of thinking is how we drive a consistent message of continuous improvement through our business. It's critical for us to align continuous improvement with our cultural goals and our North Star Vision so that we always have significant customer-recognizable improvement happening.

Process is about alignment with our core values and guiding principles. In our case, our commitment to being social implies that our processes involve freedom and give everyone a voice, but you can't talk about freedom unless you also talk about responsibility and accountability. As much as you trust, you have to validate. If you don't measure your performance, you can't be a successful social business. In sports, a high level of accountability exists because you keep score, and the scoreboard is visible to everyone. At Enterasys, we measure our business performance and communicate the results to everyone. Every quarter we have business driver meetings where each responsible head of an organization presents to the entire team their wins and losses. If you're winning all the time, then you have poor competition. In a social business, you're proud of the lessons learned from your failures because they demonstrate your ability to improve continuously. We actually boast about learning from our failures. When you're social, you can't sweep anything under the rug. Having said that, if you fail and you don't share lessons learned, then you're not part of the team. That's the "business" part of a social business.

Part of our process, which is a critical part of our culture, is the idea that we reserve the right to be smarter tomorrow – or to 'trade up' our problems. In being smarter tomorrow, we dissolve people's hesitancy to aggressively tackle an issue. This includes issues that have been around for a long time, which may have become part of people's convictions about the way we run the business. Reserving the right to be smarter tomorrow doesn't mean that what we did yesterday was wrong. We have a process for continuous improvement that revolves around thinking like a customer, which really drives our employees to consider how we can improve the business. Having the process well defined within the business and across organizations enables customer- recognizable business improvements. We've done this through our services, quality, engineering, and sales organizations, and it's pervasive throughout the company.

When we say TLC, remember that we view internal employees as customers. Why think like a customer when you're thinking about processes? When you think like a customer, you think simplicity, you think about the ease of use. While working with IT in different lines of our business we realized that unless we were able to improve the employee experience, we would not reach our full potential of improving the external customer experience. In a social business, it's all about simplicity of design and lean processes. There's a flattening of hierarchy that happens in a social business.

You're not a social business if you have multiple layers. There's the physical alignment to this idea, and then there's the organizational alignment. At Enterasys, we made a conscious decision that anyone responsible for customer support should be directed right to the CEO. When the customer tells us something—whether they're happy or they're upset—their feedback goes right to the CEO.

Customer feedback is a gift. You bank it, you open it up enthusiastically, and you share it with the organization— whether it is good or bad. When a customer is comfortable enough to tell us who their favorite vendor is and why, they've revealed to us the blueprint for success. By thinking like a customer, we develop lean processes so we can go to where the work is being done and ask the employees what their favorite tools are. If our employees don't like our CRM system, we're never going to be successful. Professional athletes have their favorite cleats; they keep their toolboxes full of tools that will ensure their success.

Because we are so focused on the experience of internal customers, our attrition rates have been untouchable. We see less than 2% attrition in our contact center, where, in contrast, typical contact centers in the U.S. have 20 to 30% attrition levels, and outsourced contact centers see up to 40% attrition.

Structure

We've already mentioned several times how committed we are to a flat structure, and that we believe in utilizing social tools to get people to chime in on ideas. The fact that we don't outsource our customer service allows us to triangulate customer issues very quickly. This is a key point that we cannot stress enough: a social business, once it identifies its core competency, never outsources it. If customer service is crucial to your business, don't trust someone else to deliver it, even if you can outsource it cheaply overseas. We pay our support technicians up to six figure salaries to pick up the phone and answer support scenarios for our customers. We know that we can find four graduate-degreed engineers in an offshore company for the same price as one of our Boston-based support engineers, because we believe that service and support is at the core of our competency and is the differentiating element of our business. A social business places a strong emphasis on the quality of customer and business partner collaboration. A social business rarely outsources core competencies. We consider customer facing functions, sales and services, as important core competencies of a social business. A social business embraces value co-creation, which means a strong desire to enable business partner success.

When you have established core values, the next logical step is to tie hard-dollar investments to them, investments which outpace the market leaders. In other words, putting your money where your mouth is. If, for example, product quality is your core value, then you should be investing more than the market standard in your products. You must spend hard dollars to make your core values a reality. A social business that doesn't spend at least a million dollars on a CRM, like Salesforce.com, is not really a social business. A social business that outsources its core competencies is not a social business.

At Enterasys, we've received a lot of third party validation. We get recognized over and over again by analysts and third party firms for our customer support. Customer service is a true differentiating element of our business. We invest in our support organization, and we see the return on it. This is a bold statement, but we believe in bold statements, as long as there is evidence to validate them. Our services capabilities are among the best in the industry. One of the anecdotal proof points we have is the number of multimillion dollar deals that have been awarded to us primarily due to the quality of our customer service and support.

Technology

We cannot emphasize this enough: technology is not going to enable you to become a social business. You must first have all the correct underpinnings in place. Just because you put on a Celtics jersey doesn't mean you can step onto a basketball court and win a game. It takes years of conditioning, the right mindset, and a lot of practice before you earn the right to put on the uniform. You need to have the underpinnings of a social attitude in order to be able to leverage social collaboration technologies. This is why, when we talk about laying the groundwork for social business excellence, technology comes last.

In subsequent chapters we'll get into technology in detail. For now, the most important thing to stress about technology is that it allows our customers to have choices. We say "fish where the fish are."

In services, customers can reach us via email, phone, or web form. They can also contact us through social technologies. We've had all of these capabilities for years. We launched our customer self- service portal back in 2005, which gave us access to customer and partner business analytics. We developed our custom self-service web portal well in advance of Salesforce.com introducing equivalent functionality.

The technology that we use has to provide value to our end customers, so when we look at technology procurement, the key takeaway is that we don't build process around the technology. We, instead, build technology around process. First we define a lean process, then we define structure, then we get the tools we need. This is why technology always comes last. Don't be enamored by shiny object syndrome!

A lot of tool and technology vendors want you to modify your process around their tools. This is an unsuccessful model. Enterasys, for one, is a high-tech company. We embrace technology and have a forward-thinking IT organization. Our CIO was voted one of the top CIO's in the Boston area in 2012. We have the ability to bring in the tools and the people that can unlock them. We choose tools that we can integrate into our process, and this translates to instantaneous business value.

The importance of technology is to accelerate your execution rate and to provide insight that you may not already have. The importance of technology is to introduce predictability and repeatability into your business, and to bolster the connections you have inside and outside of your business. Many companies believe that when you buy a piece of equipment from a technology vendor, the only way you can have access to the equipment's knowledge-base is to buy a maintenance contract. Technology vendors entice you to purchase services by giving you access to their knowledge, but we believe that when you can share your knowledge openly, when you can "mind share," you can gain market share. So we give all of our customers and partners open access to our knowledge-base, which is a database of solutions that have been authored by our engineers to help our customers better use our technology.

A social business believes that smart ideas come from both inside and outside of the company. We believe that great innovation comes not only from within our business, but also from our customers, partners and technical teams that function outside of our offices and in "the field." In the field we have professional services, solutions engineering and our technical support employees who are exposed to "real world" technology implementations. So how can we use technology to better connect us to the field? Our CRM solution can be accessed via smart phone or tablet. Our sales and service staff who live in the field can jump on their smart phones at any time to manage sales forecasts, open cases into service and support, and access our engineering database for product quality metrics. You don't have to be inside the office walls to have access to all the tools you need to run your business. Most of our service staff telecommutes, and have for years. We don't mind if they are in Alaska, India, or South Africa, as long as we can measure their productivity, efficiency, and effectiveness. We are able to do this because we're spending over a million dollars on our CRM solution annually. Giving our employees choices, and the opportunity to choose their own quality of life, gives them an appreciation of the company they work for. This is a big part of why our attrition rate is so low.

To compete and win today we need to hire and retain the very best employees with the right balance of EQ and IQ that is aligned to our core beliefs and guiding principles. The right fit is about cultural fit and skills requirements for the business. To reiterate, the most important success factors for a social business transformation, in order, are; culture, people, strategy, process, structure and technology. Winning, after all, is a team sport.

Twitter Takeaways

Social business excellence is built on Culture, People, Strategy, Process, Structure and Technology.

Culture is a shared system of values, beliefs and attitudes that shape and influence perception and behavior.

Social business culture definition is a team effort to drive ownership and to get people to champion the cause.

When defining business culture, people relate to specific personal behaviors much easier than high level abstractions.

A social business has a "constructive change" mentality which enables employees to feel safe and creative.

Three keys to social business cultural transformation; define it; live it; measure it.

A social business enables employees to recognize peers for exemplary contributions. Encourage & reinforce good behaviors.

Team chemistry matters. A social business team of employees has excellent aptitude and excellent attitude.

Social businesses live by the theme "none of us are as smart as all of us."

In a social business, you are empowered to delight your customers.

As a leader, if you're not accessible, you're not social.

Part of being social is being accessible at the highest level, and social media dramatically enables that accessibility.

A social business is always personal and transparent.

Social business is still a business. Trust, but validate.

Minimize reservations to tackle issues: always reserve the right to be smarter tomorrow or to "trade up" your problems.

A social business never outsources a core competency.

A social business always invests in its core values.

A social attitude is one that leads with humility, dignity, and respect for others.

A social business believes that smart ideas come from both inside and outside of the company.

Social business uses technology for predictability, repeatability and to enhance internal and external connections.

CHAPTER FOUR:

10 Steps to Building a Social Business

Today, most technology companies are working towards offering features within their products and services to better enable cross functional collaboration. We are living in an information sharing economy and companies that provide the right amount of data, at the right time, to the right people, will be able to differentiate themselves purely from the customer experience point of interest. This is creating a wave of interest from Senior Management teams about how to better collaborate and use these cutting edge technological tools. We see this as a challenge being addressed across all industries around the world.

Most companies fail to accomplish this strong cross-functional collaboration, and thus fail to become a social business. Here's the secret: the tools and the technology available in today's market can deliver the level of visibility that you need across varying lines of business, and these tools are great at promoting cross-functional collaboration. What prevents them from achieving business value is not a technology challenge, it's a philosophical barrier. When we present at different service consortiums and we talk about our business process of automatically notifying sales when a customer opens a case with our technical support team, what we hear from other executives is: "Why do you tell sales? Don't they just call you and disrupt your work flow and become a squeaky wheel?" Initially, that's exactly what happened at Enterasys. When we told sales that their customer called, naturally, because they're passionate sales people, they would contact us and ask us to prioritize their particular case. As you can imagine, this was mildly disruptive to our services representatives, but over time, as the value of the tool was widely recognized and sales began to trust our services representatives to do their job right. That's what full transparency is all about, and it holds true for any part of the business. Technology is never the reason a company fails; it's the use of technology. This is why we put technology last on our list of critical success factors for businesses, behind culture, people and process. Ultimately, everything always comes back to mindset and talent. Trust is built on competence and intention; if you have the intentions, but you lack the competence, or you're very competent, but have the wrong intentions, you're not going to be of value to the business.

As one of the fastest growing networking companies in 2011, Enterasys had already produced three years of consecutive top-line yearly revenue growth. Now, we have an excellent, industry- leading   net promoter score of 81, which is a measure of customer loyalty and advocacy. The net promoter score (NPS) represents a simple question that you ask a customer: "Would you recommend this company to a colleague or a friend?"

The responses are on a scale from 0 to 10, where responses of 9 and 10 are considered promoters of your business, scores of 7 or 8 are considered agnostics, and scores 0-6 are considered detractors to your business or people that would negatively promote your business and certainly not recommend your business to a colleague. The algorithm is simple; add up the percentage of promoter scores and subtract your detractor percentage scores and you have NPS. That's it. Companies can have a negative score, and generally a score over 50 is considered decent. Apple, who has a very passionate customer base and has one of the best brands in the world, has a net promoter score of 72. Enterasys' score is 81!

An 81 is a very good NPS score, in terms of advocacy. We've already stressed how important we feel customer commitment and loyalty are. We see 65% of our business coming from returning customers, and we have a fantastic employee retention rate.

Enterasys has an amazing record of growth and employee satisfaction, and we have plenty of industry awards and recognition, yet we don't have very strong brand awareness. So what's the key driver behind our success? We know that it's because we're a social enterprise. Our collaborative ethos and our customer-focused culture is what enables us to compete and win in a highly competitive, brand-driven sector. For us, the ability to leverage collaboration to humanize our business, and give our employees a voice, has helped strengthen and bolster our relationships with our customers.

Fundamentally, we believe that success comes from creating loyal customers. Customer focus is more than just the relationship between the salesperson and the customer. Creating loyalty has two foundational elements: customer experience with the product (which is why you need to have superior product quality, along with features and functions that deliver value to the customer) and a strong after- purchase relationship. It is the after purchase experience that places an emphasis on the company's customer service and support. The services team plays a critical role in a social business. In fact, all customer facing employees play a significant role in defining the company's culture and overall personality.

Customer service is a key business capability needed to help businesses obtain customer loyalty. It is important to realize that service success comes from prompt attention and quick resolution to issues. Speed of execution and minimizing customer effort are the most impactful elements of bolstering brand loyalty. In fact, there have been studies that point to increased customer loyalty when you decrease the time of problem resolution. The faster you meet customers' needs, the greater the tendency for them to be loyal, and an advocate, to your company. This is why social collaboration is important, because quickly resolving customer issues, and providing consultation to customers, is how you improve the customer experience with your business. Our ability to deliver high quality products and services is how we gain a reputation as a trusted advisor with our customers.

The benefits of leveraging social channels to deliver fast services to our customers, knowing what they need and want, is a big business benefit, but another benefit is the human voice that is representing your company. Humanizing our business gives us a voice, and that's how we scale and empower our employees. When we talk about speedy resolution, certainly it takes a cross-functional team—from service to engineering to supply chain to sales to marketing—to suit up and get in the game to deliver that quality experience. A social business has a service mindset. When we think about service, we don't just think about a service department. We think of every employee in the company being empowered to delight the customer. One of the reasons for which the actual customer service and support tends to be the most social part of the organization is because that is where the most touch points exist with customers and business partners. By working directly with a customer, you gain knowledge and understanding of the customer's specific business needs. You also gain additional insight into process improvement, business improvement, and the technology that's important to the customer.

Communication is critical in terms of coordinating and synchronizing the knowledge and the mindset that exists in your company. Without timely and proactive communication methods, a business will be unable to determine how to best meet the customer's needs. Services organizations, unfortunately no matter how good they are, traditionally tend to be in a defensive position. What this means is that they have to wait until somebody taps them on the shoulder and says, "Can you help me?" It's easy to sit back and wait for someone to ask for assistance, but in a social business you are conditioned to proactively seek out any opportunity to delight a customer; you act offensively not defensively. Here's an example:

You are a service organization studying a particular customer   contact history and then you realize that the customer is habitually contacting you for hardware failures that far exceed the expected return rates. You proactively reach out to the customer and ask them for permission to conduct an environmental health check of their entire network. You also capture forensics from their environment to try to understand why they are experiencing such a high failure rate on a product with a normally good record.

It's normal for businesses to have trepidation and anxiety about making the conversion from defensive to offensive. How can an organization go from a defensive to an offensive, proactive, preemptive mindset if it is fearful that engineering will be upset if they proactively bring up the question of product quality? A social business wants to understand the customer's needs and deliver to those needs before the customer even recognizes the issue. When we talk about social collaboration, we mean proactive communication not only with customers but also within the organization. In the above scenario, it's dire for the services team to tell the sales team that there is an unhappy customer in the ranks, and that it might be because of product quality or a poor fit with product placement. The sales department is brought in to help manage the account and find a way to recover in an effective, collaborative manner. As we've mentioned, it's important to first concentrate on internal customer advocacy, and to improve the internal customer experience before you can expect success with external customers.

At our business, we historically used email to engage with strategic issues and general collaboration, but we realized that email didn't achieve the level of collaboration we needed. E-mail was yet another tool sitting outside of Salesforce.com, which is the primary technology that we use to manage our customers' and partners' business. When Salesforce.com introduced the ability to integrate collaboration within their base technology platform, we were eager to jump in, because we understood the potential value behind this great feature.

Through Salesforce.com's Chatter social technology, each transaction is delivered in a personal manner, with a picture of the sender and embedded in the primary CRM tool utilized by the sales, support and operations organization, Salesforce.com. This personalized and integrated communication provides for rapid response and a human connection for the communication that typical e-mail does not provide.

When they think about enterprise social collaboration, many companies think social media. They're trying to figure out how to align their purpose with social sites. When asked, "How do you convince a CEO to embrace social collaboration?" Andrew McAfee from MIT replied, "Just don't use the word 'social.'" When CEOs hear the word "social," they tend to think entertainment, not business. McAfee instead used the phrase "Enterprise 2.0." The next evolution of enterprise technology is about connecting people and collaboration. At our business, the purpose of collaboration is to improve execution and enhance visibility into sharing of the best practices. Our purpose is built on the tenets of transparency, accountability, execution, and velocity, all driven by mass collaboration. It's about capturing insights from peers that are sitting on the periphery doing good work, helping us create momentum and complete projects on time and on budget, but who may not have visibility in a traditional business model. In a social business model, people and organizations are more comfortable sharing their ideas and viewpoints. In a social business, individuals realize their collaboration is good for themselves and the business. It's important for the individual to be recognized for the work they do and the contributions they make to the business. People use social media to be able to express their thoughts and opinions. They're trying to build their own personal brand; they want to belong to a community. It is the community that helps shape the company brand. They want to have followers; they want to share and they want to learn. So the goodness that exists in social media can and should exist in business too, but first, the business has to be willing to risk losing the hierarchy of command and control, and instead embrace collaboration and co-creation. It takes courage and confidence at the very top of any business to give up control. Hire the people you trust, and then trust them to do their work.

The challenge for most business leaders is to recognize the presence of the digital divide. There is no question that a divide exists in business where some leaders view technology as a distraction instead of an enabler for growth and relevance. Some view mobile, social, cloud computing, and the explosive nature of data as unimportant elements of today's information sharing in the social era. Then there are others who recognize its relevance, but their views are strictly based on the technology. The fact is that social and mobile technology is not about technology, but rather about lifestyle and choices. The adoption of consumer technologies and 'bring your own device' (BYOD) initiatives is about the need for hyper-connectivity and connection to our networks. There is a digital divide in most businesses today, and for business leaders who are on the wrong side of technology adoption, there will be a short opportunity to lead organizations into the future.

The opportunity for businesses today to compete and win is very much dependent on business leaders' willingness to embrace technology as a competitive advantage. Companies that are mobile, social and embrace modern technology like cloud computing and consumer technology are poised to improve the employee experience, and in turn delight their external customers. Digital transformation of the business mindset, processes, and culture enables growth, but you have to be willing to disrupt yourself and embrace change in a fluid and purposeful manner. Mobility, for example, allows you to conduct business with smart phones and wireless technology—where you don't need to be specifically in a room connected to a wired device. The level of efficiency gained through digitalization must be a motivating factor for technology adoption.

Social collaboration is driving mobile technology and mobile technology is driving the ability to have quality of life. The ability to connect to your peers, customers, family and friends is a choice, and the flexibility to do so means you have the opportunity to manage your time as you see fit. The paradox is that many businesses are led by those who still cling to old-school ways of thinking, and old-school management, where control and authority distort the reality of stagnation with the illusion of order and simplicity. This fear-based mentality suggests that an employee working from home can't be properly monitored and therefore not fully utilized, or that if an employee takes her laptop into the cafeteria or common area to work that she will be distracted and less productive. This is an ineffective mentality that doesn't measure actual results, but instead focuses on measuring time spent in front of the manager or in a cubical. Only mediocre managers value time ahead of results. In the social era, the desire for control is the fastest path to irrelevance. There is no safety in the status quo.

The digital divide is typically widened by a trust deficiency in a business. We often present at conferences to companies outside of the technology fray, and there is zero interest (and tremendous fear and distrust) in sharing data across the different lines of business. We are not sure if the desire for collaboration and open-mindedness is a generational issue because we see leaders of all ages embrace transparency. There is a natural inclination to think that the younger generation will be more adept at mobile, social, and consumer-based technologies. We hire and maintain a very large pool of university students within our organization, and there is no doubt that the younger people who grew up with the internet are very comfortable with data. They're comfortable with data sharing, both in personal and professional realms. The fact is that the future of work is one that consists of knowledge sharing that will be more intimate and connected than in the past. Fear, discomfort and lack of trust will only continue to shrink, and the divide will become smaller, and more heavily weighted toward people who are more socially engaged.

Becoming a social business is a significant step forward for any enterprise. There is no exact blueprint for social business transformation because of the cultural, and process variances that exist in business. But to help you think about the journey to social business transformation, we developed a list of ten steps for you to consider. We utilized these high level guiding principles to help us on our journey. Today, as we look back at our social business transformation we know that we have been successful, and yielded a profound positive impact in terms of company growth, employee delight, and most importantly customer loyalty and commitment to Enterasys.

In June of 2012, Christine Comaford, a New York Times bestselling author and a regular Forbes executive leadership contributor, co-authored a Forbes article with Vala Afshar titled: "If You Aren't Social, You'll shrink: 10 Steps To Becoming a Social Business." The article was a high-level summary of a social business, reasons for transformation, and a brief overview of the 10 steps we will cover in this chapter.

These 10 steps effectively function as a "check-list" for social business transformation. Each step should be considered thoroughly and modified as you see fit. Our intention is not to provide you with an exact recipe, but rather to provide directional guidance to help you define what matters most. We provide context for each of these steps, but you will find that mapping your transformation steps to your business will help you analyze the best approach for each stage towards becoming a successful social business.

1. Define a Meaningful Purpose

"Transparency doesn't mean sharing every detail. Transparency means providing context for the decisions we make." @simonsinek

Defining the purpose of your social enterprise transformation is a crucial step in accelerating policy adoption that is closely aligned with your core cultural attributes. At our business, we believe strongly that there is nothing more important than our customers. Defining a social business' transformation purpose around customer connection is a noble purpose that will benefit any business. We also believe that unless you are able to delight your internal customers with consistent and reliable results, you will not be able to meet the needs of your external customers. Our North Star – our company mission – is to be the best company to work for, and to do business with, based on our ability to deliver innovation, outstanding product quality, and unmatched customer service and support.

To become the best company we must embrace a culture of transparency and shared accountability. One characteristic of a company that adopts a culture of transparency and accountability is to be self-aware and present in the moment. Being present means practicing the ability to listen and engage empathetically with the purpose of learning and striving for continuous improvement. It is about serving with a passion and enthusiasm in the team's ability to make a difference. It is about keeping our eyes, ears, and hearts open so that we can be ready to capitalize on whatever opportunities may exist to help the team win, only if it benefits our customers and business partners.

The best companies, like the best professional sports teams and players, are diving for that loose ball and risking injury to help the team succeed. For us, part of this is keeping a keen eye on the industry and our customers. We recognize that thought leadership exists in the field, and that we need to be adaptive and quality driven to compete. We need to understand our customers' customer needs. Education is a key vertical market for our company. In education—colleges, universities, and K-12—our customer's customers are students. These students are highly mobile and highly social; they are the future leaders of IT that will work for us, and they are customers that we will ultimately support.

Seth Godin said, "Change almost never fails because it's too early; it almost always fails because it's too late." When we see the change that is happening at our education customers' campuses (the explosive adoption of mobility, social networking, distant and e-learning, consumer technology enabled by wireless networks), we realize that if we can't create the same environment, we will drift away from understanding and alignment to our customers' workplace. With this being said, how do you deliver innovation that has value unless you understand your customer's business needs?

Defining the purpose of your social enterprise transformation is a crucial step in accelerating the adoption of social business techniques that are closely aligned with your core cultural attributes. It is through mass collaboration that we can capture the necessary data to help us make better, faster, and more informed decisions.

2. Simplicity and User Experience are Keys to Adoption

Simplicity and user experience are keys to adoption of social communication methods. As our business determined the need for proactive communication within and beyond our organization, we realized that email is simply not the best tool to help foster large collaboration. We needed a mode of communication where it is possible to exchange information and ideas in just a few characters, express your support of something with the click of a button, and put a face to every exchange. Simplicity and personalization is a powerful combination that should not be overlooked. The user experience may be the single biggest factor in terms of the adoption of new technology.

The user experience is everything. Simplicity for us meant having collaborative technologies embedded in the tool which we use to create a single-pane of glass view of every customer touch-point. This is how our employees manage customer engagements to maintain high customer satisfaction. This meant finding collaboration technology that was embedded in our CRM solution. When choosing a medium, a key part of the selection criteria was ease of use. Simple wins. Simplicity ultimately increases your end user adoption rate. We chose Salesforce.com's Chatter, which is perhaps best described as your Facebook for the enterprise. It was simple, because it was part of our existing Salesforce.com platform, so it was easily integrated into the day-to-day work flow, which helped with adoption.

Adoption of new technology   will go smoother if it's already part of the general working environment. We have been a SalesForce.com customer since 2003, with one of the first deployment of sales and services automation in a software-as-a-service (SaaS) model. We were admittedly an early adopter of this technology, especially in the Business to Business (B2B) enterprise. Perhaps being a leading innovator of CRM technologies was an advantage for us, but we like to think the biggest advantage was having a mindset that encourages challenging our own assumptions, and then embracing change if it makes sense to do so. It certainly helps to enable new capabilities on existing platforms, and for Chatter, this was a simple decision for us to make and it certainly gave us a first-mover advantage in terms of social collaboration. We found technology that was integrated into a framework with which we were already intimately familiar and using. Is it luck? Well, it turns out that luck finds the prepared.

3. The "Social" Executive Sponsor

For a company to successfully adopt social collaboration, it needs to have an executive sponsor, an executive within the organization who is enthusiastic about embracing change and can champion it by, in effect, "being the change." A lot of companies try to do social rather than be social. Remember the acronym S.O.C.I.A.L: Sincere, Open, Collaborative, Interested, Authentic, and Likeable.

Leadership is rooted in conversation. If you take the time to listen, learn, engage and add value through conversations then you become trusted. People only trust people they like and respect. The likeability element is important because you have to trust the individual in order to connect to them. Social collaboration is about just that: connecting. When you see an executive sending personal messages about business, but also about things like "I'm at the Celtics game and I'm having a great time with my family," that person gains instant credibility. Social media is not a megaphone; it's a telephone. You can't just be communicating one way, you have to be actively listening so that when an employee says something, and that something is of value, you share it with the rest of your organization, or engage directly with that employee. If the communication is not bi-directional, it's not going to have the magic of collaboration. In order for the idea of a social business to be successfully embraced, an example must be established from the top. In some companies, that might mean that the CMO is the executive sponsor. Or it might be the VP of Services or the Chief Customer Officer. In a small startup, it might even be the CEO. The key is to find the most likeable, collaborative individual who has a large scale influence—and by the way, that might not necessarily be an executive. If the individual is not an executive, then they must be able to influence the executives – this is a must. Embracing collaboration throughout a company requires participation and support from senior leadership. You're not a social business if the CEO and her direct reports are not actively using social technologies to collaborate and engage. It takes time, energy, investment, the courage to give your employees the freedom that will empower them to collaborate, and that requires buy-in at the highest level. Always remember, leadership is example.

4. Social Adoption is a Team Sport

For companies to embrace a new way of thinking, and to form new habits, they must focus on adoption with a team sport mentality. There is only one coach, one play book and a common understanding of what it takes to win. This doesn't mean that the team captains are forced to play the game with the same rhythm and approach. Teams must be nimble and adaptive, and the planning, preparation and conditioning must be orderly and focused.

Henry Ford said, "Coming together is the beginning, keeping together is progress, and working together is success." When you're collaborating, you're coming together to solve a problem or to creatively define a potential solution. Regardless of the ownership of social media activity, it does require a team of change agents. For us, this means leveraging our extended leadership team which is comprised of representatives from our various internal customers including service, sales, engineering, marketing, IT and so forth. These are the people who have the passion and commitment to continuously strive for improvement and innovation. We addressed those particular teams and provided them with an overview of the tools, capabilities, and some ideas and guidance on how to deploy. In a social business, employees take risks and initiative. After the first few days, these new teams started to create their own Chatter lists, they started driving their own use cases and their own reasons for chatting up different events through the business in a proactive fashion. Having the right teams involved is really important.

When we deployed Chatter in January of 2010, we immediately recognized the need for senior management advocacy. Yet we also acknowledged that we are a fairly large, complex business with many products that make up our solutions. This meant that we would have to incorporate specialization within each line of business. Even within the community of services, for example, we have sub- communities that specialize in different parts of our product portfolio. So it was important for us to identify champions within a broader community representing each line of business. We also wanted to identify champions within each subcommunity. For example within marketing, you have analyst relations, press relations, content creation, and field marketing. Each of these has specific specialties. We chose a change agent from each in order to build the broadest recruitment. We called this group of change agents the Social Extended Leadership Team. We gave this SELT group access to executive management for guidance and support, but we also gave them the freedom to develop their own social collaboration mindsets.

5. Don't Overanalyze Collaboration Guidelines

When you're trying to accomplish something revolutionary, it's best not to have too many goals, or you get in analysis-paralysis mode. If your company does not embrace lean and agile processes, with great emphasis on business agility, then you are not ready for social business transformation. Part of being social is a willingness to place your trust in those involved in the collaborative effort. Hire trustworthy people, and then trust them to do the work. Below is the exact 1-page notification that we communicated to our organization when we introduced Chatter. The communication was simple to understand, and inviting.

At Enterasys, we use Chatter from Salesforce.com, to enhance communication. We encourage our employees to follow other members in their organization, as well as colleagues they regularly interact with. The guidelines we give them are: "This is a business tool, so keep the conversations business related."

We distributed a short and sweet "how to get started" guide, along with an outline of our vision to all employees. We tried to handle most of the administrative aspect of the setup in IT. For example, since every employee already had a badge photo in the system, IT was able to upload those photos into each employee's social profile. No egghead avatars! Of course, we allowed employees to change their profile picture if they wanted.

We made an effort to ensure that their first experience with Chatter was a personal one, but with minimal administrative setup work. During one of our Lunch and Learn sessions, a discussion ensued regarding senior management and their use of Chatter to talk about non-work related subjects, including topics which showcased their personalities and interests. Through further discussion, we realized that they were right. By bolstering employee's personal brands, you help bolster their work.

6. Create Social Collaboration Functional Groups

Change agents and advocates are what help you build forward momentum. As executives we may be asked to develop the vision and determine direction and destination but ultimately our people closest to where the work is done will shape momentum and forward progress. It is the front line employees, floor supervisors and managers who must serve with a passion, thus it is important to find feet on the street and talent who are willing and capable to champion the cause. To help us accelerate the adoption of Chatter we created a small group of individuals who were already proficient in Chatter, representing the various lines of businesses within our company. They were identified as folks to go to for internal support and guidance in terms of how to leverage the technology. Again, we didn't over-analyze or create strict corporate guidelines. IBM has about 440,000 employees and 70,000 contractors, and of this combined half a million employees, they have 40,000 active bloggers and they participate in 70,000 communities. IBM is another perfect example of a social enterprise embracing a culture of empowerment at the largest scale. These principles can apply to any size business.

At a company with 1,000 employees, we certainly have fairly large groups of specialized subject matter experts. One method of boosting collaboration within these likeminded and like-skilled functions is to create social collaboration groups. We created roughly seventy Chatter groups at Enterasys, sorted by various functions. Some were public groups, and some were private groups – we had no limitations Any group of like-minded individuals could band together to create a Chatter group, and there was no limit in terms of how to leverage the group. For example, a Chatter group was formed for the "continuous improvement organization." They would chat about the status of the continuous improvement program and updates, which helped build momentum around each one of those individual projects. These conversations were in a public folder, accessible to all. Anyone interested in learning about the team's progress and success could review the information. This social communication helped to break down cross-border barriers which accelerated a project's success.

The charter of Chatter was to champion collaboration and promote the work of others. The best chats, of course, are those that promote or commend the work of someone else. The important thing is advocacy, and that comes from the top, starting with our CEO, Chris Crowell, who decided that the most important thing he could do in terms of collaboration would be to share sales wins over Chatter. Chris would specifically name the salesperson, the customer, and provide details about our sales victories. The entire company knew when we won, and the sense of pride and unity helped us maintain a positive attitude. Growth starts with a mindset. Below are examples of our social chats from our executive team:

How do you convince the CEO to be socially active? The user experience is very important. Because all of this information is already in the CRM database, Chris doesn't have to data-mine to find out about these sales wins. He is already getting automatic alerts with detailed information of the sales forecast. As soon as he gets an automatic notification, in the Salesforce.com, that we have won a big deal, a prestigious new account, or a strategic vertical, he quickly chats to the entire employee population.

Chris's chats go to everybody— all 1,000 employees. In effect, he publicly promotes the salesperson for winning. At the same time, he reminds the other sales folks competing around the world that "you too can win." He is connecting the dots by connecting the people, because when Chris promotes our win of a university deal on the West Coast, an account executive on the East Coast fighting to win another university deal can now chat or collaborate with her colleague to find out how she won her new business. This creates an incredible amount of momentum for connecting people that are winning.

At other times, Chris talks about lessons learned from clients we didn't win. After all, it's only a failure if you don't learn from your mistakes. We are not using social collaboration to be cheerleaders. We open communication channels to help us grow, and sometimes that means sharing battles that we lost and the lessons we learned. You see, people don't trust perfection. People trust the truth and the truth is that we win some, we lose some, but we always compete to the best of our ability.

When we rolled out Chatter, we saw instant pickup in our sales performance in the most social region that we have, which is North America. North Americans were sharing sales wins right away, and when they saw how effective it was , it started to roll out to the other regions as well. It had an almost immediate positive impact. The design of the Chatter groups was structured into a framework that could reach the entire organization, region by region and organization by organization. Over time the other geographies followed, and also adopted collaboration to help promote best practices and each other. We were starting to become a global social business where each one of us was expanding our personal brand by sharing our individual knowledge and domain expertise. We were organically expanding our company with the same resources at hand.

7. Lunch and Learn

Lunch and Learn is exactly what it sounds like. As a social company, we find it important to fund this type of educational event for our employees. Yes, there's a cost associated to it, but the benefits justify the small expense. We make our "Lunch and Learn" fun, informal, and social. We don't want a dry classroom environment; instead we want to maintain a social buzz. In our business, the IT organization and the services organization collaborate to deliver the Lunch and Learn sessions. The faculty comes straight from our existing ELT. At each Lunch and Learn, we feature different advocates representing different departments, promoting and speaking to the best practices around social collaboration. Since we started this practice when our social technology was still in its infancy, our Lunch and Learns have helped us to figure out what works and what doesn't as we've gone along.

8. Measure Adoption

What gets measured gets managed. Any time you implement a measurement practice, you have to ask yourself what it is you're trying to measure. For us, what drives the purpose of measurement is celebrating adoption. We want to see who is active and promote those people. It is a vehicle for us to identify who is embracing collaboration. It's easy to see who isn't, because we have dashboards to measure collaboration, and it's important for us to set the tone that this grassroots movement has to be managed through positive intention. An example of the Chatter reporting dashboard is below to reference.

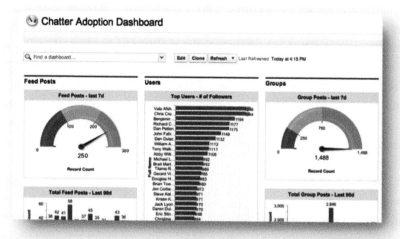

You can't force an organization to be social. They have to see what's in it for them, and what's in it for them is the recognition of their personal brand. So we recognize the top followers and the most active individuals, and we make sure to encourage them to continue on their path. When they see an executive encourage them and recognize them for being collaborative, it fuels their energy and builds momentum.

We also recognize that the folks that are successful in this area are the ones that need to lead in our training and peer-to-peer award recognition programs. The most collaborative social champions become chairpersons of our ELT. They are the individuals who help us build momentum around our social collaboration initiative.

9. Recognize Achievement

As members of the executive management team, when an employee chats about something noteworthy, we make an effort to comment on it. "Hey, great post. I like what you said, it sounds excellent." It's so simple and quick to do, and it's seen instantly by the social media mavens in our organization who are best adopting the technology. This recognition bolsters the individual's behavior and reinforces the behavior for others within the business.

The desire of a social business is to capture every win. When you are a 1,000-employee organization that's fighting to grow every day, each person must bring with them their positive and winning attitude. Some are winning battles, and some are winning wars. But there's goodness that's happening throughout the business. The broad awareness of positive progress gets lost in an organization that doesn't embrace social collaboration. The best way to maintain positive momentum is to share success stories broadly. Recognizing achievement is a key benefit of social collaboration. This is why it's important for the executive team to participate in collaboration—mainly to acknowledge the wins. Recognizing achievement, chatting about strategic new logo wins, salesperson achievements, welcoming new employees to the company, and announcing industry awards are all good examples of what companies should share with all of their employees. The entire ecosystem needs to be aware when your company wins an award.

Likewise, our IT department uses Chatter to share tips and tricks with the whole company. When we have a positive meeting with a customer, we always chat about it right away. "I spoke to the CIO of one of the largest law firms in the country and they love this particular thing about our product, and by the way, Steve, they mentioned you directly." Any time a customer gives us personal   feedback about   an employee, it is imperative for that employee to get recognized for their behavior because it promotes the best behavior in your business and helps to sustain your core cultural values.

10. Passionately Embrace Change

Social   collaboration is a fantastic vehicle with which to personalize and humanize a business. In terms of ROI (return on investment), there are certainly business benefits, because as we collaborate with each other, we're capturing insight that we didn't have in the past. There are business and performance metrics to glean from such a lean, collaborative ecosystem. Enthusiasm is a key element of embracing the shift to social, and it's contagious. So please consider a different ROI – return on interest. How much more productive and satisfied would our employees be if we expressed interest in them? An involved employee is a committed employee – no exception. Passionately embracing change and having fun while doing it is the path to success.

If you follow steps one through nine above, this last step, embracing change, will come easily. You're going to start to see your business change for the better. You're going to start to see the spirit of community building cross-functional relationships, enabling cross-functional initiatives in a way you haven't before. If you're a manager, that equals fun. And a fun workplace means that means your business is working. Things are clicking. It makes your job easier and your enterprise more successful. But, you will have to embrace the change. This is one of the struggles that some larger organizations have on the other side of the digital divide. They have to be willing to incorporate the first nine steps, as well as embrace change. If they do, they are going to see results and enjoy the journey along the way.

Juxtaposed to the above (what's not fun), is that if you're not a social business, you're not finding the wins. You're not finding the achievements of the individuals that make up your company. You're not sharing the best practices. You don't have a field community, employees that are outside your headquarters building personal trust and camaraderie with your headquarter organization—especially your executive team. There's a natural distance, like in the example we used earlier about executives passing worker bees in the hall and refusing to make eye contact. In that scenario within that sort of company culture, people don't readily share ideas or question authority in a way that may benefit the customer, the company, and various stakeholders.

One more exciting thing about embracing social collaboration: it negates the necessity for a lot of meetings that soak up time in companies today. At Enterasys, we've been able to cut way down on the amount of in-person meetings we hold. We don't need to have status meetings anymore, because our social tools take care of that function. Of course, we do sometimes still have functional meetings, where we hash out complex solutions on a white board. Some problems are easier to actively solve face-to- face, but for the rest, we have Chatter. We don't waste our time ping-ponging back and forth in meetings anymore. Instead, we use meeting time for relevant brainstorming, consensus building, and personal celebrations. This is a paradigm shift in how we spend our time.

Remember to have fun. If you are not having fun, then you need to re-evaluate your approach.

How to Know if You're a Social Business – 10 Signs

"If the rate of change on the outside exceeds the rate of change on the inside, the end is near." @Jack_Welch

There are several types of confirmation points you should look for once your business has completed the 10 steps previously listed. These 10 signs of a social business should become very apparent as you step through your transformation. The best part is that they are self-reinforcing, by the time you start to recognize the 10 signs, your teams will already feel the positive momentum.

1.   Pragmatic optimism - a social business defaults to 'Yes' and then rationalizes to desired disposition. A positive mindset of pragmatic optimism leads to an agile and change-accepting culture.

2.   Minimal layers – a social business has more of a flat hierarchy versus a traditional business structure. The distance between a single contributor and the CEO is only a few layers.

3.   Leadership is an example - in a social business, all leaders and executives are socially engaged.

4.   Music of collaboration - in a social business, all information can be accessed from the top, the bottom, horizontally, vertically, and throughout the business. Ideas are like sounds, and they should be heard through the seams of the social fabric. It is in the absence of sound that, ideas find a way to die.

5.   Social people and products - every information source in the ecosystem should be utilized to help employees make better, more informed decisions. In the enterprise, sources included people and products/machines. The network social graph of an advanced social business includes both people and products.

6.   Social integration - social businesses have integrated social channels into their processes and workflows. This means integrating social media networks into CRM solutions. Social CRMs represent the first sign of social business adoption.

7.   It's not a game - social businesses embrace gamification principles into driving employee, customer and business partner engagements. Gaming concepts, packaged into an overall CRM strategy, are key to unlocking organizational full potential.

8.   Respect but don't fear mistakes - in a social business, an idea or red flag from anyone in the company can reach the CEO directly, without a middle man, this is another example of transparent culture.

9.   Shared accountability - social businesses share complete inter-departmental performance metrics as a value added service to foster collaboration. Social businesses extend certain performance metrics to customers and partners with connection to both people and products.

10.   Reflective - a social business challenges existing assumptions and communicates the desire for course corrections or pivots in advance of actual execution.

Twitter Takeaways

Becoming a social business is as much a philosophical achievement as a technical achievement.

In a Social business, customer-facing employees are the champions of your company's brand.

The faster you meet customers' needs, the greater their loyalty to your business.

Social businesses are engaged and win championships with their offensive, not defense playbooks.

Social businesses use proactive and timely communication methods to delight customers.

A social business understands customer needs and delivers to those needs quickly, innovatively and reliably.

Social business collaboration improves execution, enhances visibility and shares their best practices.

A social business' purpose is built around transparency, accountability, and execution velocity.

In a social business, collaboration helps bolster the individual and community influence.

Hire the people you trust, and then trust them to do their work.

It takes courage and confidence at the very top of any business to give up control.

The fact is this – social and mobile technology is not about technology but rather about lifestyle and choices.

The level of efficiency gained through digitalization must be a motivating factor for technology adoption.

In the social era, the desire for control is the fastest path to irrelevance.

There is no safety in the status quo.

Defining a social business' transformation purpose around customer connection is a noble purpose that will benefit any business.

It is about serving with a passion and enthusiasm that enables the team to make a difference.

Understand your customer's customer's needs. That's when you become a trusted advisor.

"Change almost never fails because it's too early; it almost always fails because it's too late." – Seth Godin

Don't do social. Be S.O.C.I.A.L: Sincere, Open, Collaborative, Interested, Authentic, and Likeable.

Without a safe environment, where diversity of opinion is welcomed, social collaboration cannot exist.

Avoid getting into analysis-paralysis mode. Take calculated risks knowing that revolutions are won one battle at a time.

CHAPTER FIVE:

Bolstering Business Agility with Social Technologies

From Transactions to Engagement – Make it Personal

The more we speak to CIOs and industry leaders, the more we appreciate the importance of customer experience. As a part of adopting a social collaboration mindset, it's important to identify and use technology in order to move away from transactional elements—whether it's with a customer or with an employee—and toward engagements. In this chapter, we'll talk about how our own services organization evolved over time to ready itself for a social collaboration framework and mindset.

For us, technology is a key success factor, but in terms of priorities, it comes last after culture, people, and process. As a customer-focused culture, we try to emphasize a pragmatic use of innovation to deliver value and improve our "execution velocity," which essentially is how fast we get things done and how much momentum our projects take on. When we do talk about social collaboration, we say that if you're not a company with an innovative mindset, you'll always struggle with social collaboration, because innovative companies look for constant change and improvement. Our culture of innovation is fundamentally supported by innovative people who are change agents.

We moved to cloud computing software as a service model in 2003, and we will celebrate our tenth anniversary of cloud computing next year. The company we chose nearly 10 years ago to manage our sales and services processes was Salesforce.com. Can you imagine the spirited discussions we had 10 years ago, when we first talked about moving our most sensitive financial, customer, service, and support data to this thing called "the cloud"? It wasn't even in our building! As we've mentioned, one of our fundamental tenets is that you don't outsource your core competencies. Conversely, in 2003, we realized that our core competency was not in building databases and warehousing records. There are other companies better equipped to do this. We wanted to invest every bit of our energy, resources, and money toward building world class networking products and world class customer service and support capabilities, so we decided to migrate from an on-premise storage solution to a cloud-based solution with Salesforce.com. Little did we know that Salesforce.com would soon become the first cloud-based CRM provider to build integrated social collaboration technologies, but we did know that then Salesforce.com was proving to be one of the most innovative and customer focused companies to partner with.

Two years after deploying and implementing a robust CRM solution with Salesforce.com, we wanted to make sure that we had a single-pane glass view. We recognized that if we could share insightful information about how we service our customers, whether it be product quality or service quality, we could plant the seeds to produce future opportunities for more engagements with our business. In 2005 and 2006, we felt that we needed to integrate sales and engineering, and supply chain and services data in order to paint a picture describing the whole value that we deliver to our customers. We also wanted to ensure that our different lines of business could interpret that data and use it for a competitive advantage. We've already noted the example of sharing customer service and support tickets with sales opportunities. The benefits of correlating sales and service data was instrumental in co-creation of customer delight with two major customer facing functions: sales and services.

Another example was sharing product quality customer contact information that was reported in the field with our R&D, service operations, and quality engineering teams. Why would services organization want to provide field product quality information to other internal company stakeholders? So that we could ask these teams to help us paint a better picture of the plan in order to share it openly with the customer.

The services organization, for example, would say, "Dear R&D, my customer has had multiple product returns in the last six months. We know these products traditionally have only one failure per year. Would you please analyze these returns and determine the root cause so that we can communicate this information back to the customer in a proactive manner?" You see, delighting customers is a team sport, and to win, we must view customer support as a company-wide process, rather than as a department.

In order for companies to be successful at managing the customer experience, they should orchestrate their service organization as a process, not as a department. We learned that in order to achieve this, we had to develop a single pane of glass view of all customer touch points, and ensure that all the functions and employees have access to customer data. At our company, we had to ensure that everybody was using a common tool, mining data from that same tool, and importing their understanding and results back into a common technology. This limited our training time and gave us faster access to information. It created a new level of fluidity of information-sharing across multiple lines of business.

Early adoption of cloud-based applications gave us the opportunity to be more strategy-oriented. It bought us time to be creative and innovative. These were the seeds that were planted. Had we not moved to the cloud in 2003, we would not have been able to become a social business later on. If you're not a cloud-friendly business, you'll never be a social business; without "outsourcing" your data storage, you'll never have the time or resources to share insightful and actionable information socially. (The exception to this rule, of course, is companies for whom cloud storage is their core competency.) If you're just keeping the lights on and you're worrying about maintenance and testing, building data rooms and server rooms, and so on and so forth, you're not going to have the flexibility to be strategic rather than tactical.

Once we put in place single-pane customer visibility, it triggered a tidal wave of innovation back into the business. Everyone aligned to help support this, using everything from additional cloud storage, tools, and operations to common bug tracking tools. All of these new applications were launched specifically to help support our single-pane vision. Our various teams wanted to come to the table with their value-add services and data to help provide the highest level of customer experience. When you are more organized around your data and not spending all your time collecting it and managing it, you can action it. What matters to our customers is how quickly we can interpret the data and leverage our collective insight towards developing a path toward resolution. With a powerful central repository of customer data, your resources are focused on action, not collection. As much as we like to invent things, we can't invent a day that has more than twenty-four hours in it, so if you're spending the majority of your time data mining instead of understanding, interpreting, and executing actions based on your data, you're not benefitting from time spent.

You are not a social business if the information that you access can't be accessed from the very top and horizontally and vertically throughout your business. Unless you have a range of tools within "silo organizations"—for instance, marketing has its own set of tools, services has its own—it's impossible for senior executives to get trained, and be proficient enough to understand and measure business results. A social business knows that no manager is above the details. Any successful leader wants to be able to research and formulate an independent understanding of the disposition of an initiative or project. So a single-pane glass view enables all different levels within our organization to have common access to be able to use the information that we already have at our disposal.

Gamification

Shortly after we instituted our cloud computing initiative, we talked about the importance of continuing to motivate and sustain the level of momentum we needed to ensure collaboration with a balance of accountability. So we adopted gaming concepts. Today, gamification is certainly a well understood and thriving concept in businesses, especially in social businesses. The only way gaming concepts can thrive is if you're a social business. Gamification is about keeping scoreboards. In our services and support organization we introduced the concept of balanced performance scorecards in 2007. As Bostonians, we are fortunate to have championship-caliber professional sports franchises that help remind us that excellence is a choice, and winning is about team chemistry, commitment to hard work, and shared accountability. Athletic competition is second nature to us, thus the development of a scoreboard, which would help measure our team and individual performance, was a concept that was well embraced in our services organization. It also helps that we had a gritty, no nonsense culture in our business.

When we thought about gamification, we envisioned a baseball card. Every baseball player has a card with their RBIs, home runs, hits, and on-base percentages. In sports, there are specific positional players—for example hitters and pitchers in baseball—and in business, when you including customer service you create a similar dichotomy amongst the group. Different types of players have different performance attributes on their cards. For baseball hitters, a batting average, home runs, RBIs, slugging percentage, and other sets of achievements help define the potential caliber of the player – hall of famer, all-star, starter, bench or perhaps even in the minor leagues.

When we decided to use balanced performance scoring, we wanted to make sure that our employees had the same definition and understanding of what qualities make for a high performing customer support professional. We asked our employees, "What makes for a Hall of Fame services and support person?" They came up with things like, "How fast they respond to a customer in need." We did this for every part of our services organization in our company, including front-line call center personnel and escalation support engineers in our laboratories.

Every one of the attributes mentioned on our "baseball card" has a corresponding industry KPI, or Key Performance Indicator. Customer satisfaction, for instance, is an industry KPI. Case age (for cases that can't be resolved at first contact) is another KPI. The baseball card for our service professionals has up to ten different performance attributes that are scored and weighted. Together, they add up to a number that represents whether you are a "Hall of Famer," an "All Star," a "Starter," "On the Bench," or in the "Minor Leagues." The important thing is to get a group consensus on how these attributes should be scored. Much to our surprise when we first instituted this system, our services community was much more aggressive in terms of what the threshold needed to be to be for "Hall of Famer" status. We had predicted that first-contact resolution would qualify around 50%: if you can resolve six out of ten cases in the first contact, you're in the Hall of Fame, but the community thought it should be 70%. Building consensus takes time, but it's important because employees only hear what they understand. Never let a short-term inconvenience get in the way of a long-term benefit. If you rush through consensus building, you lose the sense of purpose in your community.

The performance management metric paradigm that we deployed in 2007 was cutting edge. It transformed our organization, because suddenly everyone knew exactly what they needed to do in order to accomplish their objectives. We've mimicked the gamification element of this initiative in other areas of the business as well, including with our product quality metrics. We went through the exact same process of defining what our targets were, and what our critical rates were for DOA (Dead on Arrival — products that arrive broken), for factory yields and customer return rates. We put together those targets; we socialized them; we put them in real time dashboards; we established an organization that still, to this day, gets together every single week and looks at the data. This group is comprised of engineering leads, hardware engineers, the product quality team, and the product managers.

The key to cultivating a culture of consistent excellence is to measure, communicate and adjust with a regular cadence and discipline. We developed a habit of conducting frequent meetings with the team to discuss the balance of the performance scorecard at both the group and at the individual levels. We questioned the targets, and adjusted as needed. We asked the high performers to share their best practices with the team. We redefined certain metrics along the way. The approach was a start, stop and continue mentality that helped us become an organization that was comfortable questioning our assumptions. Gamification helped our organization benchmark our performance internally, which led to a continuous improvement mindset, with a well-defined set of stretch goals for the team to follow. We have recognized dramatic improvements across every measureable dimension based on our balanced performance score carding and gaming techniques.

If you're a company that's against gaming concepts—meaning capturing performance and enticing individual achievement based on benchmarks, then you're not a social business. The tenets of a social business are, again, a culture of transparency, accountability, and recognition. If you feel that an employee is going to be upset by the fact that there's a scoreboard that shows how each employee is performing compared to the rest of the team, then you don't truly believe that transparency is key for competing and winning. It's not easy to work for a company that strives to be excellent every day, but it's also not easy for athletes to go out on the field and know that thousands of people in the audience are watching them compete. It's important that scorecards are visible. We haven't taken it to the extent where an employee can look at the individual performance of his or her colleagues, however. In the services organization, they can see their performance benchmarks against the group average and the group "best" for any of the performance categories. Degrees of transparency can be benchmarked by comparing employees with the group average and group best.

Shifting from Defensive to Offensive Service Delivery

A social business is one that's proactive in nature. There is an "offense versus defense" approach in terms of making sure you can reach the customer with something you feel is important before it becomes urgent. At Enterasys, we have developed logic to forecast the customer temperature. If we know a customer has bought a hundred of a certain widget, and we know the annual return rate is 2%, then we can predict that possibly two out of the hundred will fail within a 12-month period. What happens when we measure customer returns of that widget only six months in and find that we already have three or four returns from that company? It's a red flag. We have now exceeded our threshold of what we've defined as "excellence" in terms of quality. Or, perhaps a customer is contacting us too often with usability questions because they can't figure out how to configure or optimize one of our products. When we receive multiple contacts about something like this, we start to wonder if the product is perhaps too complex, or if we have another sort of usability issue on our hands. Customer perception of quality is our reality.

Since we are already using internal technology to measure and benchmark our employees and our different functions within the business, we have the innovative capability to profile customer contact rates. From those profiles we can make a determination as to whether things are going in a positive or negative direction. We have created predictive analytics which tell the temperature of each customer.

An important element of a social business is that when you capture customer information that's insightful, anyone who can potentially come into contact with your customer, including (and most importantly) the front line Sales and Support staff, has to be aware of it. A lot of organizations capture analytics and they determine behavior of employees and customers, but they keep this information at the management level. What's the point of not sharing information all the way to front line staff? What happens when the front line staff, who doesn't know that the customer temperature is hot, gets a call or an email or a social message from that customer and doesn't have a heightened sense of urgency because they're unaware that this may be an upset customer? Because we have pervasive CRM, and every one of our employees has access to it, temperature is the very first thing that any one of our support professionals sees when they open a case and try to service a customer.   In the CRM, the gauge is color-coded, which immediately illustrates to the service professional the expectation of the customer. This is one element of the "offense versus defense" mindset: utilizing information in a social business to proactively delight and improve each customer experience.

Customers certainly know that with any high tech product, there are going to be issues of some sort, but they would much rather be engaged in a proactive way than a reactive one. Customers put immense value on being respected in this way. When we talk about transparency and becoming a trusted advisor, a lot of it has to do with the way we engage with our customers. By using Salesforce.com CRM analytics we are able to proactively engage our customers based on predictive analytics capabilities. We use predictive analytics to analyze product field quality and to engage appropriate engineering quality resources to determine if preemptive actions are required based on field data. Our quality data collection tools provide us with a very advanced capability of proactively engaging customers. Having this level of data helps us make timely, informed decisions that we share with customers and partners in order to demonstrate our culture of transparency and accountability. This is how we build customer and business partner trust, and, over time, loyalty and commitment. Without transparency, we cannot achieve our ultimate goal of having a customer for life.

Data is in the Rear-View Mirror, Theories are on the Front Windshield

Clay Christensen explains that with all the data we have, our information is still all from the past. In order to be successful, it's vital to have theories about the future. You don't have to have data about the future (you can't, actually), but you can formulate theories based on the data of the past. Predictive analytics extract data from the past and then ask you to theorize about what the customer temperature is going to be in the future. So, if you thought two out of one hundred widgets were going to come back in six months, and instead you see seven come back three months into the measurement period, what's your best prediction of the customer temperature? They're probably upset, but they might not voice it to you, because indifference is awfully quiet.

We're just as concerned about quiet customers as we are about those who are express their upset vocally. There are two types of people: walkers and talkers. Some people never complain about poor service, whether it's at a restaurant or when they invest in the services of a company such as ours. They simply never come back. We've all had this sort of experience at a restaurant we didn't particularly like. Perhaps we didn't complain to management, but we never visited that restaurant again. In our service organization, we are delighted when we get feedback from a customer because it's a gift. It's the walkers that concern us, which is why we have predictive analytics. We want to service the customer in a proactive manner. In order to do this, we have to have a desire to collaborate, be accountable, and take ownership. "Dear customer, it's our problem until it's no longer yours." Remember, when we say "customer," this applies to the external and internal people that we serve.   When we say "customer," we're talking about anybody that depends on a service. Internally, if you depend on a service and you don't get it, you may not be able to do your job, thus you may not get paid.   In effect, all customers are paying, in some capacity.

Proactive reporting and predictive analytics guide you to better communicate with the customer.   When the gauge predicts a red temperature, it's time to proactively contact the customer.   There are two gauges we show to our frontline customer service staff.   One is a read-only gauge that can't be modified. The other is a read-write gauge, which can be modified.

If the system predicts that a customer is in the red zone, it then shows as read-only to inform the frontline staff of predicted condition. However, if a manager contacts this customer and gets a real-time read, then it's at the manager's discretion to assess the actual customer temperature. The manager might ask the customer, "We know that the number of widgets that are coming back is greater than what we anticipated, so we want to conduct a study and find out what's going on." If the customer tells the manager, "You know, I'm glad you called, because I'm really upset with you. I'm about to go buy from your competition," the gauge is going to stay in the red, but if the customer says, "I appreciate you giving me a call; I understand the failure conditions are due to our environment and I'm actually very happy with you. Thank you very much," the manager might decide to set the gauge to green or to yellow.

When a front line person logs in, she immediately looks at the two gauges, and if both are red, she reaches out to the customer immediately. But if one is red and one is green, she knows she doesn't need to escalate the situation quickly. The temperature gauges provide predictive visual indicators, but behind them is operationalized information. It's not just about throwing information out there, you have to tell a contextualized story, and that story has to result in a change of behavior.

We utilize this system each and every day. We have learned how to engage customers from an overall sensitivity level, which includes analytics on their buy patterns and cycles. This allows us to prioritize the way in which we use our service inventory for sparing strategies. Our ability to profile our customer contact has advanced beyond capturing call center contact and also includes product usage profiling. Today, we are connected to our customers via public social networks and private networks using our CRM solution. This live and active remote monitoring capability enables us to correlate network activity to the features and functions that are in use. More importantly we can now leverage active network profiles and correlate user and application activity to help us provide consultative services—in real-time—to help our customers realize the full potential of our solutions.

Markers for Better Predicting Success

One of the most significant benefits from being able to generate collaborative predictive analytics is how we leverage and action these data points in the sales organization. We are able to look at sales forecasts to determine where to focus our efforts to win the business. If we have two opportunities, one with an existing customer and one with a new customer, and we don't know much about either, we would traditionally bet on the existing customer because it's obviously an easier sell.

Access to historical information allows us to build a correlation engine and profile for each opportunity with a set of markers that helps us make a more informed decision. These markers can include deal size, since we know our sweet spot, won deals averages, the age of the opportunity, and industry and other helpful characteristics. A weighted sum algorithm can be used to establish a predictability score based on pre-determined weights associated to each of these markers. For example, a sales opportunity from a university or college would be given a higher weight than a financial institution, given our historical performance selling into these markets. If you ask a set of questions to determine what kind of a bet you are looking to make, then you can formulate a theory using data from the past to assess how hard you need to emphasize, collaborate and work on winning an opportunity.

We assign an integer score to all our sales opportunities. We aren't trying to predict our revenue—although, this prediction engine is unbelievably accurate, and such accuracy is one of the side benefits that has come out of our prediction system. We've developed amazing accuracy—sometimes within a 1-2% range —as we've refined our algorithm over time. More importantly, though, is our ability to assess the value of an opportunity. Based on the win probability score that we assign, we can formulate regression analysis and view historical performance, and then assign a dollar amount realization based on predefined thresholds.

What is important to remember is that the predictive engine of our sales forecasting solution, and the mathematical modeling capability, is not the main benefit to the organization. The main benefit knows what questions to ask in the presence of these markers. The extended and shared visibility gives us the ability to ask the right questions at the right time. The biggest benefit is expanding the sales organization to be inclusive of the other lines of business so that we compete as a team of one. This is why predictive analytics really is one of the key elements of a social, collaborative business and why we utilize them daily at Enterasys. Having a scoring mechanism on sales opportunities helps drive our supply planning process, so we stage inventory for deals based on the likelihood of each deal closing. That particular algorithm drives a tremendous amount of operational activity every single week around how we plan to maximize revenue and overall profitability for each venture.

The chronological summary of our use of enterprise technologies to help bolster a culture of transparency began with our decision to move to the cloud in 2003. We created the single-pane glass view in 2006. We introduced gaming concepts, a balance scorecard, and a crowd-source performance model in 2007. In 2009 we talked about predictive analytics in order to benchmark and look at historical information, and to determine the degree of engagement with customers. Salesforce.com then introduced Chatter at their Dreamforce event in San Francisco in September 2009. We were at that conference and we thought, Facebook for the enterprise? Will this work? Certainly several of us were skeptical about the full potential and benefit of social collaboration in the enterprise. But, of course, a small pocket of us starting using it and soon realized that the instantaneous access to information, and ability to collaborate, could actually really help us transition from a transaction-type behavior to an engagement-type behavior within our company. Chatter introduced context, personalization, and connections that could be widened outside of a line of business and outside of the abstract (and detached) construct of email. It added a personal element to a short, communicative type of dialog. Because it was less formal than email, Chatter quickly became a way to socialize our business by early 2010.

Machines as Part of the Social Fabric

So far, we've talked a lot about the basics of social tools, specifically in terms of internal collaboration and customer engagement, but we haven't really touched on how a social business interacts with the external world beyond direct customer relationships. Vala Afshar—co-author of this book—and several other members of the executive team were early adopters of Chatter within Enterasys. In the business-to-business environment of early 2010, our use of social collaboration technology was mostly limited to Chatter. Vala was chatting about industry publications that he was reading, customer stories, initiatives, and changes that were coming into our business, along with general things he found interesting.

One Monday morning, he saw an email come in from Twitter with his name, picture, and the bio "Chief Customer Officer at Enterasys" from the Twitter alias @ValaAfshar. He thought, "What clever spam!" The account mimicked what Vala would have created himself, had he created a Twitter account—which he hadn't. He was puzzled. He received this spam as he sat in a sales meeting, anxious to contact Twitter to report a potential security threat, but then suddenly he was approached by a friendly peer. As he sat in the meeting listening to the sales presentation, the CIO, Dan Petlon, tapped him on the shoulder and said, "I just want to let you know I created a Twitter account for you." Vala said, "Dan, why would you create a Twitter account on my behalf?" The CIO brought up a CRM dashboard regarding company Chatter usage and said, "Guess who has the most followers in the company?"

Vala had no idea that he was by far the most active Chatter employee with the most followers in the company. Dan quipped, "It puzzled me, too, because you're not really all that interesting, but you take the time and energy to share what you think is interesting and important for the business on Chatter. I want to remind you that everything that you share, even if it reaches every single employee here, is only going to reach about a thousand people. So for the next month, do me a favor. When you find something that's interesting, and it's not specific to our business or confidential, why don't you tweet about it?" Dan then showed Vala the basics of Twitter (thankfully, it's not terribly complex).

In a company that lacks a well-known brand, Vala thought, why not try Twitter to see if I can make a difference? What if every employee with a passion to serve was given the opportunity to bolster the company's voice? Dan's logic was very sound. He started to connect to certain technology publications through Twitter, including technology and networking publications like IDG (computer world, CIO.com, network world, etc.). Vala manages a good portion of Enterasys's business personnel, so he is interested in the principles of business leadership, and therefore he follows publications such as Harvard Business Review, MIT Sloan Management Review, Fast Company, the Wall Street Journal, Economist, Alltop, and Inc. All of these organizations have Twitter accounts. It didn't take more than a day or two for Vala to fall in love with the fact that all the information he had been reading, either in print or on the web, was now being delivered to him in real time.

"Accident is the name of the greatest of all inventors." Mark Twain

He was in listening mode at first, but eventually, Vala decided to put something out there in a tweet. He used the Twitter hash tag #leadership, and instantly saw how people begin to connect and share. Suddenly, all of the beautiful things about internal social collaboration were starting to seem possible outside of Enterasys's internal Chatter. Because Vala saw the power of real-time information coming from analysts that he connected to, publications that he was reading, thought leaders with similar positions, and the competition, he soon became amazed by how much valuable information was being delivered on a silver platter via his Twitter stream. A light bulb went on, and he realized that this same technology could eventually be used to connect Enterasys's engineers with their hardware in order to communicate more effectively, twenty-four hours a day and seven days a week.

Until that point, engineers, whose job was to diagnose and test hardware, relied on the hardware to communicate information to them in a very traditional and constrained manner. You see, the engineers needed to have access to the hardware, which meant they need to be near the machines – typically in the R&D laboratories – in order to securely and seamlessly connect to devices. But at the end of the day, they would go home, leave the machines and their diagnostics behind, and have to wait until the next day to look at the information that the switches, routers, products, and the machines were producing. Meanwhile, Vala was seeing that his Twitter account fed information to his phone or tablet all day and all night, every single day, wherever he would go. He thought, "Why can't we convert this complex machine language to social language?" If he could make that happen, engineers could then get technology messages delivered to their devices from anywhere, anytime. ISAAC (Intelligent Socially Aware and Automated Communication) was born. ISAAC came from the idea of leveraging social collaboration internally and then expanding our involvement with public social technologies. Chatter and Twitter both contributed to the idea of inviting machines to be part of the social fabric.

The Birth of Twitter

Vala's motivation for using Twitter was simple, "How can I get our company name out there?" Based on preliminary research of social media case studies, the usage showed that companies used social media to market their products and services, improve alignment of internal resources to market needs, collaborate with customers, and increase their ability to capture competitive intelligence. Vala jumped into this fray with purpose and vigor, and this inspired other leaders at the company to get on Twitter and develop their own voices.

Fairly quickly, three things happened:

1. We suddenly started to do a much better job of marketing our company's capabilities and business success to the public with a broader awareness of our company culture, people, products and services.

2. Our company brand gained a human voice; the collective output of our social employees was resonating in our social networks, and we taught people the name of our business. We were in the news more, and the press, analysts, and most importantly our customers began to reference us using social networks. We started to actively participate in Twitter chats and share stories that would help our customers and business partners. We tried to listen and engage instead of sell, sell, sell. It wasn't about us; it was about technology, the market, and our customer's success stories. We felt we had established thought leadership amongst our partner and existing customer install base, but this was the opportunity for us to share with anyone who was giving us a chance to be heard. We were grateful and enthused.

3. Validation by industry analysts and the press was fueling our social networking momentum. If you have a business that's customer-centric, people want to hear about it. We constantly share customer stories that get re-tweeted by influencers, analysts, and celebrities. This has helped a lot of people outside of our business realize the value of our opportunities.

Although   the above benefits blossomed   from our induction into the world of Twitter, very few of those things would have happened without the basic foundations we already had in place. The right culture and the right people will ultimately determine your social networking success.

It's difficult to create a winning attitude, but it's more difficult to sustain a winning attitude. A winning attitude is not just swagger at the senior management level; you have to maintain and cultivate that winning attitude with every employee. Part of our collaboration journey has been inspiring our employees to feel good about our company—the organization they're part of—and their colleagues, because every day they're reminded of the wins. There are certainly painful lessons that we've learned, and when we understand a root cause, and figure out how to fix it, we share what we learn. In a culture of transparency, it is okay to make mistakes as long as we don't point fingers at others, and so long as we make sure we correct and learn. When we started using Twitter, our motto was, "be interested first, and then be interesting." If you're interested enough, you will be become interesting over time.

It's a critical human desire to be part of a winning organization that has a high-performance mentality. At Enterasys, we've been able to have a high performance business for a long period of time because we have a winning   mentality, despite our underdog status. Because of social media, the sharing of wins, and the sharing of very positive business elements, we are able to maintain our winning edge.

As we said before, underdogs win because they know they can. Underdogs win because they work harder and smarter to gain a competitive advantage. But it's also important to have a sense of humility and a healthy case of paranoia. When you're overly confident about what you do, there may be a lack of discipline or a refusal to collaborate. An underdog, however, has a heightened degree of due diligence that drives their desire to want diversity of opinion.

Please remember, no matter how big and successful your company is, there will always be smarter people on the outside, than on the inside of your business. For this reason alone, it makes sense to adopt an open mind and an open heart. Collaborate willingly and scaffold your value. That's how you compete and win in the information sharing economy.

Twitter Takeaways

A social business feels like a small town - people know your name, doors are open, lights are on.
Dear company, there will always be smarter people on the outside, than on the inside of your business.

Collaborate willingly and scaffold value. That's how you compete and win in the information sharing economy.

Underdogs win because they work harder and smarter to gain a competitive advantage.

Brand = Talent. by @Tom_Peters. | Hire and retain the very best and invest in their success.

All the data we have is from the past. To be successful, develop theories and then execute.

Every day, good ideas are being killed by people who find safety in the status quo; there is no safety in status quo.

Reflection is good. Look to the past, just don't stare. What you do NOW will shape tomorrow.

Collaboration starts when you are willing to share your performance with others. Collaboration takes courage.

In a social business, a single-pane glass view of departmental performance exists to all stakeholders.

CRM powered automated workflows and service level agreement reporting are keys to collaboration success.

Customers build relationships with our people, not products. Empower your frontline to delight.

In a social business, information is accessible from all levels of the organization, from executive management to frontline staff.

The key to cultivating a culture of excellence is to measure, communicate and adjust with a regular cadence and discipline.

Organizational and employee balanced performance scorecards are most effective to bolster service quality.

A social business uses gaming techniques to motivate and improve employee performance.

Gamification is not a game. Well-designed gaming principles in business can significantly bolster performance.

A social business uses CRM-powered predictive analytics to proactively deliver customer service.

Social analytics, derived from people and machines helps social businesses differentiate service quality.

Social business leaders share what they believe, not what they do. Understand the "why" drives engagements.

CHAPTER SIX:

Case Study – Our Social Business Examples

In this chapter we will present two Enterasys case studies in a more formal, detailed way. The first will speak to how we implemented social collaboration technology to help bolster our service and support capabilities. The second case study is our Continuous Improvement Program, driven by our use of social collaboration tools to enable processes whereby departments could successfully deliver value added services to internal stakeholders.

Case Study One: Implementing Social Collaboration Technology at Enterasys

We believe that leveraging social collaboration technology is helping us save a considerable amount of money. We're estimating north of one million dollars per year is saved by leveraging Salesforce.com's Chatter and our services cloud implementation.

The Challenges

Certainly, as a premier global provider of security—wired and wireless—and software solutions, we're always looking to enhance our customer relationship management system in order to give us more robust visibility among our global clientele. We serve customers across seventy countries around the globe and we process tens of thousands of service transactions on an annual basis, so our support team is highly engaged with our customers. It's important for us to be able to leverage the transactional insights that we already have in order to further improve our understanding of our customers' needs.

We had already developed our single-pane glass view of customer touch points using our CRM solution, thus it was a natural stepping stone for us to think about how we could leverage internal collaboration using the customer data that we already had. A challenge for us as a company that lacks brand recognition and has a significantly smaller market in a very competitive space, is to have innovative solutions, strong product quality, and exceptional service and support. At the same time, reducing costs and introducing efficiencies is a challenge for any company regardless of its size.

We looked at our existing processes and noticed that employees had to manually enter information using email or, at one point, Microsoft SharePoint technology in order to collaborate. Using tools outside of our principle technology, our CRM solution, was impractical. Our challenge was to maintain an economy of scale and efficiency, while at the same time improving the employee experience. If you ignore the employee experience you're ultimately ignoring the customer experience, and we still needed to deliver strong service and support.

The Idea

We had built automated workflows and service level agreement conformance using the CRM. Because of this robust technology foundation—which was already being used by all of the service and support personnel, as well as product management, marketing, and engineering—this was naturally an area where social collaboration made sense as the next step.

Certainly, part of the challenge was shared accountability via shared visibility and the opportunity for us to meet our customers' needs at their time of need (execution velocity). We already had the sales cloud (sales automation logic that's used for forecast management) with Salesforce. com, and we also had their services cloud, which helped us catalogue information by product family. In early 2010 we decided to take advantage of the Salesforce.com Chatter implementation as well.

The Details

Implementing Chatter was initially meant as a way for departments to share useful information in order to achieve transparency and greater consistency within the business. We leveraged sales forecasting capabilities by licensing all of our sales employees to manage their forecasts within Salesforce.com. We added big machine quoting tools and enhanced the program using Salesforce.com's application exchange program. In combination with some custom development work that we had done internally, as well as using the ecosystem consisting of Salesforce.

com partners and developers, we were able to create a sales forecasting capability that leverages social collaboration throughout the business.

One of the specific advanced uses of our Salesforce.com Chatter implementation in sales is the ability for us to create social forecasts. As account executives manage their forecasts and make changes and updates to their forecasts, the system will automatically notify the various stakeholders based on the changes, and we can quickly determine whether the changes are positive or negative to the forecast. With positive changes, we can easily engage with "liking" the status or commenting. With movement that's in a negative direction, we have an opportunity to determine how particular lines of our business can help course-correct the forecast.

With Salesforce.com's service solution, we've implemented online case management, which enables each customer to log into our Enterasys intranet through a web portal and view all of their active cases, make case updates, and have total visibility in terms of the lifecycle of their issue. As a reminder, we're in the business-to-business space, so it's not unusual for customer and partner contact to be complex in nature.

Even though we strive to resolve customer issues 70% of the time upon initial contact, there is always an inventory of open cases that move through the various lifecycles of service and support, and thus it's important for our customer to have visibility. We created mobile applications so our customer could contact us using their smart phone or tablet in addition to social channels where a customer could use Twitter, Facebook, or Chatter on their mobile device. We extended additional capabilities which allowed customers to log into our web portal using a mobile application that can be easily downloaded from the iTunes store (there's even an Android version). This kind of access gives our customers, who are mobile, the opportunity to understand how we're managing cases, and to look at our progress summary reports.

We've also built training applications where a customer can become certified in Enterasys products and technology and engage social channels as a means of communicating with us as they're going through training sessions. This gives them the opportunity to connect with instructors, and have a guided curriculum as they're learning about our solutions and technology. We use support tools to improve the transactional customer experience with our customers and partners. One of the very simple enhancements that we added to our mobile application and our social web interface was the opportunity for the customer or partner to click a button and request a discussion with a manager or director-level support person. We have internal service level agreements that guarantee that a manager or director, or support personnel will be in touch with the customer upon request, and that's certainly a great example of our desire to make sure we're accessible.

The Results

By using the services cloud and social collaboration techniques, we have developed predictive analytics. This gives us the ability to determine the customer temperature based on their contact history and temperature fluctuations over time.

Stakeholders—who could be at a director level or higher—are apprised of customer engagement opportunities based on temperature. We provide partner access to all of these web-enabled contact capabilities, so that our partners can also leverage our technology, our visibility, and our ability to understand the customer temperature and then appropriately decide whether they need to get involved and/or guide the process.

A social business practices transparency with all stakeholders, removing the element of surprise. As we compete in the mid-market space, not all of our partners are giant companies with massive budgets and unlimited field resources, so it's important for us as a social business to take the tools and technology that we have and extend those capabilities as much as possible, thereby enabling our partner's success.

At Enterasys, Chatter-specific implementation to drive collaboration occurred within both service and support. We originally implemented Chatter to understand the activities that were going on within our company, not just in the vertical parts of the organization, but also horizontally and within the seams. We began to clearly see how single contributors from one function (like service or support) would and could collaborate with contributors from other functions like R&D, engineering, product quality, and so on and so forth. All of this collaboration could be collated and compartmentalized for the specific customers and cases that were actively being worked on. The contextual element of the collaboration was quite easy to see, because it was always aligned to a particular case, a particular problem, and a particular enhancement.

We created many Chatter groups company-wide, but in the service and support organization alone we had roughly forty, which sounds like a lot because it is. Groups were created based on different functions within the services organization. For instance, we had a professional services group, a training and educational services group, a field engineering group, and a technical support group. When you look at any one line of business (whether it's marketing or engineering or services) in a $400 million dollar, 1000+ employee enterprise, you will see multiple disciplines that make up just that one function. So we created sub-groups to make sure similar projects and similar initiatives could be captured by the individual functions within services. We also created groups by technology. When a customer contacts us, given the fact that we are a manufacturer of technology with a very strong, robust, wide portfolio—from switching technology to routing technology, wireless technology to software security or software management—it makes sense that we have different classes of products within each technology group. We have higher commodity, less expensive products at the periphery of the network, and we have multimillion dollar core switching and routing solutions. There are a lot of opportunities for segmentation by class of technology, product type, and various functions within services.

One might question the point of slicing and dicing collaboration into various groups given our ultimate goal of complete transparency, but it's important to reduce noise. Social systems that are functioning well are inherently noisy. We want people to have the freedom and empowerment to voice their opinions and what they have learned; you want them to openly discuss mistakes and accomplishments. We also want to make sure that our people don't get overly distracted or, worse, tune out. That's why having different groups within the services organization working on different projects and with different objectives makes sense. Yet, at the same time, we want to have an overarching group—a superset—so that if one of the leaders of the organization wants to share a crucial, company-wide piece of information, she knows that it will be heard, and that it will benefit everyone.

For us, one of the key advantages to social collaboration is that we've reduced our broadcast emails by nearly 80%, and that number continues to grow. If we want to talk about a new initiative and it is specific to a pricing issue, we only chat it to the operation team responsible for pricing. We know that our front line call center staff will not necessarily be interested in the back and forth collaboration on a pricing initiative, but once the pricing has been finalized and agreed upon, we then chat to the entire community at large so they have a better understanding of how we're competing in the business. Every initiative requires hundreds, if not thousands, of back and forth conversations in order for us to achieve consensus and finalize the direction and destination. The advantage of grouping is quite clear, and our Chatter implementation has made all of this possible.

We've enabled products to be part of our social network in the services business, and we're now able to connect to our customer networks through a private social cloud. We capture information that is both actionable and manageable, which leverages machine-to-machine social collaboration. We've created an unparalleled degree of efficiency and effectiveness by using this solution. Our annual savings is north of $1,000,000 and is the result of increased efficiency, and stronger customer relationships.

Our high net promoter score speaks to our greater visibility both in the pre- and post-sales process. When we speak to our customers, they describe what a graph of their communication with other vendors looks like: a high peak prior to sales, followed by a drastic negative slope as soon as the sale is finalized. But with Enterasys, they say, a graph of the attention they get would show a spike even after the sale is complete, with a constant increase in the level of collaboration that takes place between the client and Enterasys.

This is a very important characteristic of a social enterprise; it is consistently engaged with the customer before and after a sale, and continues to adopt the mindset of the customer for life. You need social intelligence in order to determine how you can stay engaged and using content that's relevant to the customer at each point of said engagement.

If you're engaged but you're not delivering information that's meaningful to your customer, whether it's in a reactive or proactive manner, you will lose the customer's interest. At Enterasys, we create process enhancements in the service and support operations, including coding capabilities, configuration capabilities, and analytics, by virtue of the social element resulting in being tied into both the service and support cloud.

We have improved our marketing capability, including our lead generation ability. We launched a lead generation program almost by accident after recognizing a simple fact about our new system: we can easily gain valuable insights from our customers' needs and proactively suggest new solutions. For instance, if we're listening to a customer describe their legacy network capabilities and they mention features and functions they wish they had (and we have those features and functions to offer them), we can use that insight to immediately engage internally with our service organization to capture those requests and communicate them to our sales organization.

Using social collaboration techniques embedded in our CRM, our service and support professionals actively listen to our customer's technological needs, and then quickly chat about new opportunities while in the process of delivering service to the customers. Within a short time period—just a little more than twelve months—our services organizations have been able to produce millions of dollars of sales opportunities through leads that were communicated to our sales organizations using Chatter technology.

We have carefully and methodically created an entire lead generation process that, over time, will transform our service and support from a cost center to a profit center. We realize that hundreds of thousands of interactions back and forth with customers in our service organization create an unbelievable wealth of knowledge in terms of what our customers have in their networks, how they are using their networks, and what potentials are being left unfilled that could be answered with our product portfolio. By enabling our support organization to collaborate with the field personnel, we are able to bolster our lead generation capabilities within the company.

Using Chatter, we handle thousands of cases per week, and we have been able to measure and reduce our time per case by approximately 20%. Time per case reduction has been a result of collaborating with domain experts throughout ecosystem in real time. When a customer contacts us about a particular solution or technology, that inquiry leads to a behind-the-scenes collaboration with multiple engineers. The customer gets a one-to-one experience, and behind the scenes, using social collaboration, we have created a training opportunity.

One of the advantages of social collaboration in services is the ability to transact and train simultaneously. Traditional training models have the support trainee leave the seat to sit in a classroom, listen to lectures, case studies (like this one!), and training materials. They would be given dense knowledge bases where they could search a particular inquiry and look for documented solutions. All of these are effective and they're still in use at Enterasys, yet another strong training tool is in-process training. While a trainee is processing a customer request, they can simultaneously collaborate with more experienced, available agents who can lend their own knowledge and expertise, on the fly. This training practice has reduced our time per case by 20%, including our case resolution time. Don't forget that 70% of all our support contact is now resolved at first contact.

Collaboration within the business has also helped us become more of a trusted advisor with our customer, and our customer satisfaction scores have increased, which has boosted customer commitment and loyalty.

A social business understands that a satisfied customer might still purchase from the competition. Loyalty and commitment are driven by execution velocity—making sure that we deliver the best solutions at the right time, and collaboration has enabled us to do just that. Our overall first-contact closure rates have increased by 19%. Prior to reaching that 70% milestone for first contact, we were roughly in the fiftieth percentile. If a service personnel is stuck on a call answering a client's question, the ability to quickly chat with other experts while the client is on the line provides an immense boost to each service representative's ability to fix problems in real time. Instead of relying only on their own knowledge and a static database, they now have a hundred other service and support professionals, some with much more experience, at their disposal in an instant. This would not be possible, by the way, if our service was outsourced.

We increased the capacity of our support staff by more than 13% using social collaboration, which improved our call abandon rate by 20%. One of the key measures in the contact center is what percentage of time the customer abandons the call when they have to wait too long for a response. Improving abandon rates is critical to maintaining the loyalty and trust of the customer. By decreasing our resolution time on cases, we naturally create more available agents for new cases. Instead of spending more time servicing customer A, we increase our efficiency in servicing customer A and move on to customer B.

You can score this way if you're suited up and in the game. Even if you have an excellent service and support organization, if they're stuck servicing a customer when another customer needs their service, it's a fail.

No matter how appropriately you're staffed, if you can't manage spikes through mass collaboration, you could have customers waiting for support and find yourself unable to respond. The phone is still our number one connection to customer service, and we suspect that phone support will continue to be the most popular channel through which customers contact technology companies, especially given the complexity of supporting enterprise class networks. Nonetheless, we have reduced our talk time by 15%. In the future, mobile video contact, sourced from smartphones or tablets and social channels like Google+, will become the preferred contact channel into B2B and B2C support centers.

For medium to large size contact centers, every minute of reduction on talk time can produce many years of efficiency. Today, roughly 60% of our contact with customers is phone support. On average, our talk time (the amount of minutes we spend on the phone per transaction) is roughly fourteen minutes. Reducing our talk time by 15% equals many, many minutes of reduction across tens of thousands of engagements. Collaboration remains key to all of this. Social businesses look forward to speaking to their customers. Social technology is not used to deflect customer phone calls, at least not at Enterasys. You fish where the fish are; if the customers want to speak to you, you speak to them. If the customers want to tweet to you, you tweet to them. If they want to engage with Chatter, that's where you are. Social collaboration simply provides another channel. It gives the customer another choice in terms of engagement and connectivity.

As much as phone contact will continue to be the predominate preference for our customer—and from a global point of view, as social begins to drive mobile—there's no question that in the near future there will also be more and more contact initiated from customers through social networking channels. In a social business, telecommuting becomes the norm and, as we've mentioned, if you don't believe in telecommuting as an option for your organization, you aren't really a social business. Telecommuting is not an entitlement, of course, it's a privilege, but social businesses recognize that the employee experience is what drives the customer experience. If the support employee has to sit in a car and commute for hours every day to come to a physical call center, instead of being at home with access to world class tools at her instant disposal, she is not going to be quite as happy. This is why we're spending millions on technology at Enterasys in order to delight both our internal and our external customers.

Case Study Two: Our Continuous Improvement Program

Our second case study is about creating a continuous improvement methodology within Enterasys. We utilized social media in order to source the best practices and ideas through tools such as Chatter, LinkedIn, and Twitter. This has been a continuous improvement effort that we are still finessing today. We'll talk about some of the accomplishments at the end of this case study, but for now, let's talk about the challenges that led up to it.

The Challenges

Our business has a heritage of long product lifecycles, and our customers expect that our product will last eight to ten years in their network and beyond. When a competitor introduced a lifetime warranty, we knew the expense of maintaining long lifecycles would soon be shouldered by our company, instead of by customers who pay for hardware maintenance. We had many processes that required adaptation to this new world of lifetime warranty. On top of the lifetime warranty, a third party component issue found its way into a legacy product line. The combination of these events required immediate action. We needed to implement a continuous improvement system that aligned directly with the top-line objectives of our business.

We wanted to drive cost enhancements and overall quality enhancements among our customer base. We had to align our resources around this mindset of continuous improvement. We needed to implement a continuous improvement framework, and we needed to implement a quality data system around that framework. From there, we needed to be able to implement a process in which we could affect the business and change behavior within the cross-functional organizations based on that data and the continuous improvement methodology.

Of course, it's important for a technology company to have the highest perception of quality; quality is non-negotiable. When you have a critical infrastructure element such as a network, downtime is not an option. People expect that they will have, at most, a few seconds of network downtime per year. This is a significant challenge that we welcomed.

The Idea

We first put forth a continuous improvement proposal which was truly a wide open framework. Projects could be brought to the table by anybody in the organization, as long as they aligned directly with our business needs. Naturally, we used Salesforce.com and Chatter as our social communications mechanisms for this initiative. We collaborated on ideas through Chatter and provided status reports within the Chatter interface. This allowed us to quickly create a clear understanding of each problem, and how a proposed solution would drive improvements in the business. Before we'd jump into a solution, we would socialize the idea, define the desired results, and discuss how the project would impact that desired result. We did all of this through our social interface. We communicated often, and provided daily updates to small groups through our social tool. This way, we got quick business results from small teams that were able to make decisions quickly. Having a social tool, such as Chatter, embedded in our business, increased results in a matter of months instead of a matter of years. At the same time, we kept a large population within the company involved in a "Master Continuous Improvement," or a Chatter group with close to two-hundred participants. Everyone could see the status of the teams, so it was a very transparent approach to tracking progress.

The Details

Our executives joined about half a dozen quality-related and management-related social discussion groups on LinkedIn in order to share ideas., We also utilized tools on Twitter such as "tweet chats," where people with a common interest or subject share ideas. We used these forums as brainstorming sessions to get hundreds, and in some cases thousands, of people involved in a single conversation. Having direct feeds from critical thought leaders in the industry, on an array of subject matters, and with all sorts of expertise, allowed content to be delivered right to your door. This is one major benefit of social tools like Twitter and LinkedIn. Quick access to all of this data creates effective thought leaders because aggregated collective data triangulates directly to business needs.

To date, we've had approximately two hundred employees—20% of our total company—participate in our Continuous Improvement Program. We've had over thirty-five teams form, execute their project, and graduate. As this book is being written, we have about fifteen active teams still working.

We attribute the success of our Continuous Improvement Program to the following three critical success factors:

1.   Providing high-level support visibility. We tie each core project to our key business initiatives. The first key to success is ensuring a high level of support visibility, which is greatly enabled by our social tools. Leaders propose projects, create very detailed scopes, and share them throughout the industry (outside of our company) using social media tools such as Twitter and LinkedIn. This encourages thought leaders throughout the industry to benchmark the projects for us.

2.   Maintain process credibility. We have to follow the process, focus on results, and operationalize said results. Having the ability to promote our projects and celebrate their success is an absolutely critical element to getting operational results, and social tools really help us unlock that ability. We use consistent training at Enterasys in order to keep people up to speed on the best practices that we utilize to enable continuous improvement.

3. Motivate employees. People need to be motivated in order to want to help change the business. When employees have the opportunity to get involved with a project, define their desired results, see progress that's tied to business needs, and then get recognized by company management at the end of the program, they get tremendous affirmation. Being able to deliver business results in a social fashion, and being able to have those results communicated and recognized   throughout the business via chat groups, breeds success. We need to continue sharing and advocating approaches. Our use of social tools significantly enables this.

The Results, So Far

Our Continuous Improvement Programs reach across several core functions of our business, including engineering, services, quality, supply chain, and finance. We mentioned one: our quality data closed-loop system. Last year, we were awarded two Manufacturing Executive Leadership 100 Awards (ML100 Award). One award was for our quality data automation, and a second for "next generation leadership and culture" for our continuous improvement focus and the subsequent positive business impact.

Social businesses have to be transparent. Our closed-loop data quality management system allows us to have real-time data for all of the quality aspects of our products in a single-pane glass view so we can see all of the product quality factors that affect our customers. This enables us to make smart decisions, which best impact customer perception of our quality. Some of the dynamics in our business that create continuous challenges include the extended lifecycles of our products, lifetime warranties, rapid technology cycles that change quickly over time, and having a distributed supply chain. Our closed loop quality data management system allows us to address each of these challenges by providing real time data to make product lifecycle, product design, and product support related decisions.

We have data connections with our global manufacturing and repair sites, which transmit information from our "in-process" test equipment for real-time, detailed information on our factory processes. We also have real-time connections to both our Enterprise Resource Planning system (SAP) and our Customer Relationship Management system (Saleforce.com). All of this data is collected and presented in one systematic set of dashboards, and these dashboards allow us to analyze trends from our customer, from our manufacturers, from our suppliers, and enable proactive actions to improve product and process quality.

This proactive management of our field population of products and factory processes enables an empowered staff that looks forward to solving problems, and is not overwhelmed by data collection. Our engineering teams can action the data versus collect the data. This was a major paradigm shift that allowed historic levels of efficiency with our quality resources. The implementation of this tool was very quick in comparison to the scale of the project. This speed of implementation was due to our structured continuous improvement process, and the result of hard work from the focused cross-functional team.

We now have real-time dashboards that show every quality statistic for each of our products, and the data is updated every single day. Because of this, every engineering leader and support manager knows exactly where all of our products stand. We feel confident about promoting our quality to our customers with conviction behind our numbers.

Our engineering product quality data enables us to educate our customers, and advise them on the right approaches to take to best support their network. This helps us and our customer implement the most resilient network designs. This was a core objective of our Continuous Improvement Program. With the ability to quickly action our product quality data, we have been able to make major strides in improvements to critical product quality metrics and customer quality metrics. We have reduced our overall return rate on our highest-volume product line by 41% based on the business and supplier process changes driven by our continuous improvement program.

Many of our products have a lifetime warranty, and because of our reduced return rate, we have realized a 50% reduction in our overall warranty reserve per unit that we ship. This has a direct bottom-line impact on our business. It means that for every unit we ship, we can put more money directly into our pockets. This is in line with our profitability and customer goal of better quality perception.

In order to win customer loyalty and trust, a social business approaches customer service as a team sport. If you only rely on the services organization, and you don't focus on product quality, you're going to lose the game. If you only rely on quality initiatives, but don't think about innovation and adding feature functionality to stay in line with your customer needs, you're also going to lose. Much like a team sport, a successful social business is one where you have innovation, product quality, and service excellence. Unless you collaborate, you're going to fall short.

Transparency across Enterasys has allowed us to experience some of the value-added services to our internal and external teams – a hallmark of a social business. We've provided sales leads based on quality projections and the age of inventory, data for which we now have perfect insight. We've improved manufacturing process, repair policies, and testing requirements for our products, all of which have driven significant yield improvements. We've created rapid failure analysis by integrating with our Salesforce.com platform. We've seen reductions in overall return rates and higher speed of resolution with customer issues.

One of our most complex products, which has 17,000 discrete components when assembled, has seen a 76% improvement in return rate over the last eighteen months. Our products, overall, have seen only about a 25% return rate since we deployed this tool, and simultaneously had a continuous improvement methodology. We've seen a tremendous amount of bottom line business impact, which has the ripple effect of success breeding success, and it's all built on the shoulders of the social tools we've implemented. Our business alignment and socialization through Chatter, and the validation of best practices—mining of thought leadership with tools like Twitter and LinkedIn—have created a significant level of improvement that is continuing to provide bottom line results.

Through network design and product reliability, we are able to achieve the highest industry standards for network uptime. Our particular approach to continuous improvement, supported and bolstered by our social tools, has really driven this result, and, in turn, this type of result drives our business to the next level.

Both of these case studies attempt to illustrate the real benefits of social collaboration throughout our business. Did we start this journey knowing first-hand that we would gain such enormous business benefits? The honest answer is no, but we did intuitively know that the benefits of an open and collaborative environment could only improve our business agility and quality-driven processes.

Twitter Takeaways

If you're ignoring the employee experience, you're ultimately ignoring the customer experience.

A social business practices transparency with all stakeholders, thereby removing the element of surprise.

Collaboration is not easy but it's important. Don't allow a short term inconvenience to get in the way of a long term benefit.

A social business can significantly reduce expenses by leveraging collaboration technologies.

A social business can cultivate a culture of transparency by utilizing collaboration technologies.

Social collaboration technologies in business help humanize interdepartmental transactions to engagements.

Social analytics helps businesses improve their ability to deliver proactive customer support.

The new net promoter score is the social promoter score; ask: did you promote, to whom, and what were the results?

Integration of social business intelligence and CRM is the effective customer experience management strategy.

Social customer services allow our frontline employees to collaborate in real-time to deliver faster service.

The key to customer loyalty is resolution speed. A social business delivers faster service.

With the right intentions, you don't need permission to lead.

Quality of our products and services is defined by our customer's perception. Solicit feedback for continuous improvement.

Trust your gut. Be data driven, but don't ignore the potential benefits in absence of clear ROI.

Try it, fix it, and try it again. Fail fast.

In a social business, departmental performance metrics are shared across the lines of business.

Social collaboration is based on the ethos of value exchange, not value extraction.

In a social business, performance metrics are shared with a push versus pull communication model.

In the social era, knowledge sharing is the only way to scale our competency and trust factor.

In a social business, mediocrity has no place to hide.

CHAPTER SEVEN:

The Sign Reads: "There is No Lifeguard Here"

In 2005, W. Chan Kim and Renée Mauborgne wrote a book called Blue Ocean Strategy that proposed a new paradigm of business behavior. A quick synopsis of their theory is that the future of business is in creating new areas—blue oceans—of uncontested market space. Rather than continuing to compete over the same arenas, forward-thinking companies look for new ideas and revolutionary ways of thinking. For us a new way of thinking started when we recognized the explosion of mobile and social technologies and the growing complexity of managing networks with pervasive adoption of consumer technologies.

We needed to consider the user experience, and lifestyle, of today's modern worker; and it was this mentality, guided by the deep desire of differentiation, that we took to heart. This was the impetus behind the invention of social machine communication and the creation of ISAAC.

It's hard to ignore the megatrends that are driving the purchasing decisions and organizational changes in business today: mobility, social collaboration, cloud computing, and big data. The amount of data and information that's being produced by mobile devices, social media, and applications that are in the cloud is enormous. The user experience is a critically important consideration because of the complexity avalanche caused by all of the technologies being introduced in business. There is a growing consumption gap between what products and technologies can theoretically offer to businesses versus their actual use. The concept of the consumption gap was introduced by J.B. Wood in his book titled Complexity Avalanche – Overcoming the Threat to Technology Adoption.

Refer to the illustration below as we define the consumption gap.

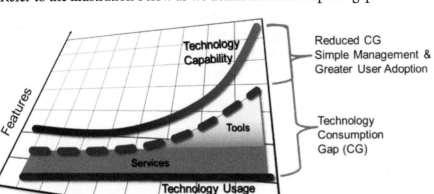

As a technology vendor, it is important to think about how we can improve the user experience with our products. If we can focus on executing pragmatic innovation, guided by simplicity of design and use, we can compete and win. The customer experience is everything and it must be inclusive of the brand, products, services design and functionality. Our ability to simplify and improve the customer experience is a core element of our sustainable growth strategy.

"If you're not the simplest solution, you're the target of one." - @boxhq CEO @levie

A September 2012 IT World post written by Mr. Dan Blacharski covered the ISAAC innovation and its impact on reducing the consumption gap. Mr. Blacharski wonderfully captured the value of social collaboration to help improve feature adoption. A summary of the post is below:

Closing the consumption gap: Making use of the features you have – IT World, by Dan Blacharski

The emerging model for software development has come to a point where it must transcend the underlying technology. Some of the most interesting software companies never make it, because they develop useful technology but that's where they stop. The companies that succeed are the ones which go beyond simply rolling out a feature-rich piece of software, to positioning it as a part of the business model. Instead of asking, "How does this technology work and what will it do," the more appropriate question now, is "How does this technology change how we do business."

Moving from simply providing functionality, to changing how companies do business on a meaningful level, means addressing what Vala Afshar, Chief Customer Officer at Enterasys, refers to as the "consumption gap."

"I'm looking at an iPhone in my hand right now," said Afshar, "and as I stare at it, I realize that I probably only use one percent of what this thing is capable of. We're selling enterprise switching, routing, and wireless technology, and we're adding new features and functions to our solution. So, if I think about the consumption gap that exists, which I'll define as the current use of technology versus the capability of the technology. If you plot those two lines, you'll see there is a divergence of the lines over time."

Afshar notes that the most effective way to reduce that consumption gap is to increase feature adoption. Some companies approach this task through customer service or training. "A business can reduce that consumption gap by building a collaboration environment, and let technology enable this effort." That's where the idea for Enterasys' ISAAC was born.

Enterasys realized that addressing that consumption gap means providing an interface that fits into a social context, and with natural language. ISAAC allows users to establish a two-way, natural language dialogue through social media, between human and network.

Network management by itself is a fairly ordinary function that everybody has. It's not disruptive, and it doesn't change how people do business—but when you add in this natural, collaborative mechanism, everything changes, and then we get back to the concept of transcending technology and really developing a new business model that changes, and improves, how the business works in a meaningful way. What ISAAC does is takes a big step towards improving the state of the art of human-to-machine communication through a familiar, and highly accessible, social media interface. It lets IT manage network devices via Twitter, SalesForce Chatter, or Facebook, in real time.

On the back end, what ISAAC does is take complex information, and parses it into natural language; and then establishes a secure, two-way social interface so that IT can ask questions and issue commands. At the same time, network devices can send messages to alert the IT manager that action needs to be taken.

Naturally, most IT managers, when told that they can communicate with network devices through social media, the first question is, "How is that going to be secure?" Like any cloud-based system, security is built-in of course, with role- and message-based security, and two-factor authentication. The 500 high school buddies you have on Facebook aren't going to know you're having a network issue.

There are two compelling things about ISAAC. First of all, it brings in a deep and fundamental change in the business model by shifting network management to a much more intimate and social two-way dialogue. Beyond that, one need only look to the future a few years to see how the potential of ISAAC could go far beyond network management, bringing in simple and inexpensive ways to control smart homes, HVAC systems and other devices.

Technology, and the people who use it, have historically not always been at the same level—and technology frequently gets ahead of itself. Today, with companies like Enterasys making those rich features easier to access and use, the technology gap will decrease.

What good are new software releases with hundreds of rich features if you don't know they are there, or don't know how to use them? With products like ISAAC, we will see a future where companies can release even more features—and have those features delivered and implemented in a natural, interactive front end so that the consumption gap is reduced. The natural language, two-way, social dialogue between humans and machines/software represents the next technological leap forward in changing how we work.

It's Not About Technology; It's About a Lifestyle

Imagine a world where information technology administrators and professionals could securely communicate from anywhere using the tools that they know best. What do young IT professionals know best? They certainly know social media, and it's everywhere. One sixth of humanity is on Facebook and Twitter alone. That's over one billion users combined who are not only social, but mobile, and ultra-connected to their networks. In business, the social network is expanding every day to help enhance employee and user experiences. Mass collaboration also improves business agility with respect to understanding and meeting customer needs. Most importantly, a social business is able to co-create value with engaged and committed customers and partners

Certainly, the social collaboration CRM led by Salesforce.com is an example of a pervasive, simple- to-use method of human networking that serves the business. For us, delighting our customers by using mass collaboration (via social CRM) is a driving factor yielding continued company success and growth. However, the fact of the matter is that the human network is only a small portion of the interconnected network entities. The future of connected network entities – less than decade, according to most analysts' predictions - will favor machine to human connection in a 7 to 1 ratio.

What is driving the explosion of growth of mobility in business? It is social collaboration that started with texting, and now includes massive social networks that are vibrant inside and outside of business. When it comes to the proliferation of mobile and social users, the devices that they're using to connect to networks are only part of the "ecosystem."

Social CIOs and businesses recognize that mobility is not just about technology; it's a lifestyle. It's about choices. It's about the freedom to be able to do your work from wherever you are. Social media has the capacity to provide an increased level of productivity and flexibility. It also provides a level of intimacy that is needed in business to help humanize employee and management interactions within the company to better serve the customer and partner community.

Today, mobile devices such as laptops, smart phones, and tablets, are the primary means used to connect to the internet. Recent reports have said that two thirds of Americans are buying smart phones; and when they choose a phone, they're not choosing just a standard phone, but one equipped with applications, web access and other advanced functions. On top of that, we're seeing the growth of cloud computing, which is delivering a flexible consumption model with an unparalleled scale. All of these cloud-based applications are enabling businesses to do more without the need to have capital investments in infrastructure. As long as they have access to the internet, they can have access to business performance applications.

As you keep all this in mind, imagine the possibility of increasing management efficiency by providing ubiquitous, secure access that is always available, with the customizable, natural, and local language that social media offers, to help connect humans to machines as well. The natural evolution then becomes machine to human, and finally machine to machine communication via social networks. The genesis of building social products, which we introduced in 2011, was the notion that humans should be able to communicate with machines using the tools that they have on hand.

The fusion of social, mobile, and cloud technologies translates to a user experience and innovation velocity that is rapidly accepted and implemented by our customers. This means that our customers are most comfortable using social networks like Twitter, Facebook, and Salesforce.com's Chatter on their mobile devices. Wireless devices, where you don't have to be connected to a wired office to be able to conduct your work, are the norm now. In 2011, we publically announced that we were going to simplify and increase customer adoption of our own company's products by giving our customers the capability to use a common interface to monitor and talk to our enterprise networking machines (switches, routers, and wireless devices) through ISAAC.

In a typical customer environment, you have hundreds of thousands of machines networked together, and registered to a network that's managed by a central management station. Your network management machine extends the visibility and control of your network to an administrator. This central network station also monitors machine performance and messages that are sent by the equipment.

With ISAAC, we created a social media translator that turns machine language into automated human communication. This social media interface runs on top of our management station. Any time a complex, traditional machine message comes into the management station, it is converted into a "natural language" command as a chat, or a tweet, or Facebook message. This social media interface also translates incoming messages, from the mobile user connected to the public cloud, into commands the management station can understand and transmits said commands to the targeted network devices. There is bidirectional communication to and from the machine, and a public cloud enables the customer experience magic that differentiates us from the rest of the market.

For example, in our IT organization, we have created commands that describe the health of the network so that our IT administrators can use Chatter on their mobile devices to gain insight into our network's health throughout our thirty offices around the globe. They can also communicate back to the network in the same way. It's no longer necessary for us to constrain IT to a desktop computer, in a network command center, or personal office. Our IT organization can see and control our global enterprise network using consumer technology, and a UI that is accessible to over one billion people – the social web.

When a help desk receives a customer call regarding poor bandwidth use on a mobile device, our IT managers can send a command to find the user. We can then chat to our device, and our device will chat back the location of the user, the network that the user is connected to, and all the various forensics about the user. In a mobile environment, you're typically connected to a wireless access point with an IP address, and there's other information that you can leverage in order to understand connectivity and performance issues. The fact that our IT administrators can use social media on their mobile devices to conduct complex IT troubleshooting, and have that information converted to social language then delivered back to the mobile administrator, is an incredible example of improving the user experience.

We are utilizing social collaboration with machines in order to delight our customers. Gartner recently noted that by 2014, more effort will go into redesigning existing applications to make them social, than will go into deploying new social software products. When we started designing and building ISAAC, we wanted to know if we could tweet to our network IP infrastructure and have the machines tweet back, and now we are successfully chatting with our own enterprise network. It has become more and more clear to us that this functionality will ultimately define the next generation of social enterprise. You are not a social enterprise if your machines are not social; and the full potential of social enterprise is achieved when both people and machines are part of the social network graph. That is the genesis of ISAAC, and our first swim in truly blue waters. No other technology vendor is delivering social machine technologies in the enterprise networking space, and our head start positions us to lead the charge on social business transformation and thought leadership.

It is very important for a social business to identify customer thought leaders who are innovative and looking to gain a competitive advantage by leveraging the latest technology. Fortunately for us, the most successful market that we support is education, in which some of the best and brightest CIO innovators exist. Our very first ISAAC customer was Phil Komarny, the CIO of Seton Hill University. Mr. Komarny is one of the best, and most innovative, CIOs in higher education. Komarny's vision of the future mobile, social, and cloud-enabled campus sets him apart from most CIOs in education. Phil and his IT organization were the first in the US to provide Apple iPads to all students, faculty, and administration. He has grown his wireless network by 400% in two years, reduced his IT budget year after year, and maintained the same staffing levels, while absolutely delighting students and faculty. The retention and recruitment numbers are another benefit resulting from his thought leadership. When Mr. Komarny and his team deployed ISAAC in June of 2011, Seton Hill University became the first in the world to manage their enterprise network via Twitter. Mr. Komarny, Vala Afshar, and the chief technology analyst from IDC spoke about the implementation in a Network World webcast in 2011 with the use of case examples of ISAAC.

In the web cast, Crawford del Prete, the Chief Analyst at IDC discussed the use social analytics to improve business agility and performance. In the Network World webinar with del Prete, the panel talked about ISAAC, the social revolution, and the benefits of our technology.

During that rich hour, we had analysts talking with customers, we did a demo of ISAAC, we chatted from a tablet, and we showed just how the machines provide exact user location to help us troubleshoot network problems. You can see a recording of this demo at: http://www.enterasys.com/products/ISAAC.aspx Please take a look at the video to better understand our social machine technology; watching it will give you a comprehensive overview of ISAAC's capabilities.

Machine-to-Machine Communication

Today, mobile users are receiving chats from networks telling them when there's a wireless connectivity issue that might be suboptimal. Yes, the machines (wireless network) monitoring other machines (mobile devices, connected to networks) are letting the people (network IT administrators) know when something might require human intervention. In 2010, we started with the people-to-people social collaboration at Enterasys; in 2011, we invited machines to our social network graph, and began collaborating and communicating in the most seamless, customer-friendly manner from a user experience point of view.

Now, in 2012, we see machine-to-machine collaboration via social media technology as the natural next step. We're already implementing Chatter technology and our network management software to make this next step happen. We are now monitoring mobile users that are—for example—looking for the signal strength of the wirelessly connected user, and, based on the data, determine what actions are necessary. Our network management team can develop watermarks in terms of signal quality markers that define suboptimal use for a mobile user. They can configure our machines and wireless access points to let us know when there is a connectivity issue with a mobile user. This means that the machines detect behavior that may be anomalous, they can chat to us via our CRM cloud.

Because the social technology we are using, Chatter, is a Salesforce.com module, it is a seamless fit. We are already inside the Salesforce.com CRM sales and service cloud conducting business. We can now parse the Chatter content, and pick out data to create service tickets in the Salesforce.com services cloud. We have the social collaboration technology, and the customer relationship management services automation capability. Within this same framework we can take chats and automatically produce help desk tickets. When those tickets are created, we have automated work flows that inform the user, and engineering and customer support communities of each event.

Traditionally, when a human customer has a poor experience with a product, they will contact another human at the help desk and describe their network condition and behavior. The help desk will then record and capture as many forensics as they can in order to escalate the case to a vendor or an engineer to troubleshoot and find potential remedies. A typical lifecycle of a traditional support case has multiple stops, with a series of manual (human intervention) steps along the way. Our machine-to-machine communication, via social public network – Chatter – is greatly increasing our ability to process the contact lifecycle. The customer is now spending zero time on tactical IT work, and spending more time on operational and strategic needs of their business. We are also spending less time administrating service and support inquires by adding artificial intelligence to boost our social intelligence and service delivery capabilities.

Our ability to increase service execution velocity is largely due to our social channels, which are integrated into our CRM frame and inclusive of both people and machines. In the ISAAC scenario, machines are invited to the chatter stream, and because the chats are happening within the CRM tool (Salesforce.com), as soon as an anomalous behavior is detected by the machines service tickets are created automatically. The first time an actual human is invited to, and aware of the situation is when the user is informed that there is a remediation plan already actively in play. The networking group and the engineering teams are simultaneously informed that there is something they may need to investigate.

The natural evolution from people-to- machine, to machine-to-people is now transitioned into machine- to-machine collaboration, which goes back to the primary goal of delighting of customers and measuring customer loyalty. We've said that customer loyalty is a function of how fast you can answer a customer question or resolve a customer scenario. The fact that we can have machines collaborating with each other, and communicating through a social network, expedites and increases the speed of our resolution, and that is certainly in the spirit of proactive service delivery. Because machines and humans are now connected by a social channel in a dynamic and integrated CRM framework, the result is faster identification, and faster notification and resolution; the positive impact of all this is a better user experience.

You're not a social enterprise unless your social channels are integrated into your business processes and workflow. The integration of social collaboration technologies in a customer relationship management framework is a true signature of a robust, mature social enterprise. Looking back over the last decade, as we have adopted a cloud-based CRM gamification in the enterprise, the ability to leverage predictive analytics, the removal of interdepartmental boundaries, and the single-pane glass view, it becomes clear that it has all been powered and delivered through our Salesforce.com CRM. As of now, in 2012, we have extended all of this to our machine network via ISAAC, which has brought us a whole world of opportunities in terms of how we can use machines to provide us with more dynamic intelligence in order to make better, more informed decisions about our business.

Using Artificial Intelligence to Create Social Intelligence

Certainly we recognize that the transformation of our business into a social enterprise is still in its infancy. We're just starting to peel the potential layers back in terms of our full social potential, and we're going to be working with our customers collaboratively to guide us along the way. We're also working with industry pundits—like Michael Krigsman, a CEO and prolific blogger for ZDNet, and a Wall Street Journal technology and business process contributor, who has been covering the IT industry for three decades—to help shape our social business transformation strategy.

The "blue ocean" mindset is defined by the desire to be the first in the industry to do something revolutionary: to disrupt conventional approaches to solving customer pain points in a manner that is unique and relevant. This way of thinking is not revolutionary because of shiny technology motivations, but rather, it is revolutionary in terms of improving the customer experience. When a company adopts a blue ocean technology and an innovation roadmap, it is important that they connect with innovative thought leaders—customers, business partners, technology strategic alliances, and industry analysts—who can provide case studies to validate and shape your product roadmap. In "blue oceans," we don't have market intelligence competitive analysis to look at. There are no features, nor functional gap analysis, and there is no competitor to compare ourselves with. It takes a higher degree of creativity and collaboration to think about what ISAAC will look like one year, two years, or five years down the road.

As a company that's leading in the social enterprise space, we have to leverage our customers and analyst organizations to shape our decisions and create a technology roadmap. The blueprint that we're trying to develop speaks to best practice implementation, cloud computing, social collaboration, and explosive growth consumer technology. Always work with your customers to define your vision and strategy, because thought leadership exists in the field. There is no better way of improving your ability to innovate than by getting closer to where the work is being done. Identifying trends, like social, mobile, and consumer technology in the enterprise must be identified as early as possible in order for companies to maintain their innovative edge.

Consumer technology in IT is one mega-trend that led to our "blue ocean" network management innovation and ISAAC. The fact that smartphones and tablets enable our customers and employees to conduct business in an efficient and cost effective manner is what draws our social technology roadmap. The explosion of IT consumerization and cloud computing is the fuel that drives the ISAAC innovation. ISAAC is the fusion of all those capabilities that enables you to do your job using mobile, social, or cloud-based technology, and you don't need yesterday's supercomputer in order to do it.

Today, we're inviting customers to be part of our social cloud via Chatter. Chatter was initially introduced as a private social collaboration cloud within the enterprise—only and always within the enterprise. But in 2012, Salesforce.com announced the ability for companies to invite individuals outside of their networks into their Chatter social networks. In a private, invite- only fashion, you can have customers and partners from outside of your organization be part of your social collaboration cloud.

Inviting customer and partners to our Chatter social networks is really interesting for us because we realized early on that if we could invite our customers to be part of our social network, it would give us an opportunity to invite our customers' machines to join our social network as well. Why would we, as a service organization, want to connect customer networks to our social network? Our social network happens to be our customer service and support CRM system, which is how we manage our customers; thus the same benefits we had when managing our own IT infrastructure by using Chatter to communicate to our internal network, can now be extended to our customers.

When a customer network is having issues that need to be understood, analyzed, or remediated, their machines can now chat to us through a secure, private Salesforce.com Chatter cloud. This is done using a public cloud infrastructure, so our customers don't need anything but internet access to connect. They don't have to buy another piece of hardware; they don't need to expand their network. All they need to do is connect their network management system on site, through a secure public social cloud, to an Enterasys cloud. Now, as the machines chat to us about the happenings in our customer's network, we can parse the forensics, create a service ticket, and inform the customer whether we need to investigate or send them a replacement part. We now have the ultimate level of simplicity and proactive service delivery because the people at our customers' sites don't have to do anything; the network is doing it for them. It's artificial intelligence enabling social intelligence, which enables proactive, timely service delivery. In a nutshell, we are using artificial intelligence to create social intelligence.

Alan Turing, who's considered by some as the godfather of computing, developed the Turing Test and wrote a seminal paper in 1950 that sought to answer the question, "Can machines think?" His test involved a human and a machine responding to questions, with a blind observer attempting to determine whether it was the machine or the human that was answering each question. If the observer was unable to distinguish, the machine passed the "Turing Test," meaning that the machine could "think." In July 2012, Mark Fidelman wrote an article for Forbes titled "Social Machines: How This Company is Using Artificial Intelligence to Create Social Intelligence," and in it he asked whether machines can do a better job than humans at protecting a company's network and specifically mentioned our methods:

"Enterasys seems to think it's a smart idea worth pursuing. They've created a solution called ISAAC that is using social media and mobile apps to protect their customers' networks. But this solution involves more machine driven intelligence than human intelligence to generate process and share information."

Delivering secure messages from a network infrastructure via Twitter, Facebook or Chatter in a user's local native language is the important distinction. Today, most of this technology and infrastructure is manufactured in the U.S. or bought by companies that are based in the U.S. Although you have networks in other countries around the globe, you're communicating with commands that are English commands. When you can map these complex English commands to local languages, the level of user experience will certainly increase the adoption and desire to do business with a company that can provide that solution. One of the advantages of inviting our machines into the social construct is that we have made our products more integral to our customer's business. It's harder to displace a product when the usability is far better than any other product in the market. As the Forbes article goes on to say, with network security as a priority concern for CIOs, it's incredibly important to ensure that this explosive use of mobile devices ensures the highest level of availability and security.

The most effective way of maintaining a secure, available network is to leverage all information nodes in order to understand the behavior of your network. But, it's the machines that are capable of delivering the large volume contextual information that we need to ensure network availability. Therefore, the notion of self-supporting networks is an important element of ISAAC's capability. We provide this level of security and availability by ensuring that when machines provide us with forensics, all insight is provided in a mobile, social, cloud-based fashion. The users, administrators, and all of the humans in the social enterprise are moving along the mobile social trajectory. We can proactively detect that a user has sustained, let's say, a low wireless connectivity and today this is now identified and delivered to us through a Salesforce.com Chatter message. This early detection is critically important to improving our execution velocity.

The support that we're delivering to our customers—and the crucial fact that the entire lifecycle is machine-to-machine without human involvement—has a bottom-line benefit. At Enterasys we compete against Fortune 100 to 500 companies. We sell our products and solutions to both large and small businesses throughout the world. One of our core markets is the small to medium enterprise. The customer profile of a typical small to midsized enterprise organization is one with a limited staff, including a limited IT organization. Even if you have enough people on staff, the explosive nature and complexity of technology will always be a challenge in terms of training. The cost of making sure that the IT organization has the appropriate skill set to maintain and deliver the solutions that the business needs can be large in both time and dollars.

By adding the ability to create a machine-to-machine service lifecycle, we have alleviated the need for our customers' IT staffs to spend time doing tedious transactional work when the machines can do it for them. We have given our customers and employees the ability to use machines as a means of receiving alerts and updates, and to simplify transactions. These real-time inputs from our products improve the customer experience with the product and improve the operational costs to deploy and manage our products for our customers.

So where do we see this going? We have customer CIOs who are innovative thought leaders that have connected their machines to Enterasys through a social public cloud, and we certainly have the humans—both at our company and our customers'—connected and collaborating. As cool as it sounds to have the machines taking care of the product serviceability, the fact that we have everyone collaborating throughout the organization—from the CIOs all the way to the network engineers—means that we are gaining insight into the type of work that's interesting to our customers and the projects that they have. Most importantly, they are more comfortable sharing insights with us that we would never have gleaned in a traditional call center ticketing system. CIOs are communicating with us more richly through Chatter because they realize that by doing this work, they are embarking on a journey of blue ocean innovation, and they see themselves as thought leaders embracing the social mobile cloud. CIOs have to stay relevant, and part of staying relevant is being strategic and delivering business value.

If you're a CIO and you don't want to be a part of a social enterprise, you're going to have a very limited career. If you're not a social business, you will shrink, not just from company market share, revenue, and growth perspectives, but in terms of your career trajectory as well. Customers are social, and the need for collaboration is quickly becoming the only way to gain market share. At Enterasys, we have our customers and their machines connected to us through a private, secure, social network. What's our vision going forward? We'll illustrate this with a scenario:

Let us assume that you have two different universities (University A and University B) with dissimilar skill sets in terms of their IT staff, but similar needs in terms of a network infrastructure. Both universities have the same exact e-learning initiatives, the same mobile students, and they're both trying to connect faculty and administration to the student population. These schools have exactly the same business challenges and needs, but when it comes to skill set, domain expertise varies between the two. University A has domain expertise in wireless technology, but is lacking in switching technology; University B has unbelievable switching architecture, but they are not strong in wireless technology. These are social customers who are willing to connect their networks and themselves to Enterasys. Our plan would be to invite all of the people and the machines of both universities to join a common social ecosystem.

By having all these individuals as part of the larger ecosystem, questions and needs would get met by different domain experts, whether they require troubleshooting, optimization, or crucial skill set. Collaboration makes for amplified experts. Again, this idea comes from the belief that there are always smarter people outside of your company. Our ideal is to create an environment where both feel safe and secure, and can collaborate with each other.

Inviting our customers to cross-pollinate and leverage each other's talents is a construct that enables a synergistic business model, and provides a collaborative business value to our business and to our customers. By the time we present at Dreamforce in September 2012, we'll have a dozen universities and colleges connected to us through a private, secure Chatter collaborative. This machine-to-machine connectivity is just one of the ways in which Enterasys is swimming alone in a blue ocean.

We're also leveraging Salesforce.com, our CRM solution. Today, we have predictive analytics that help to manage our sales forecasts. Our sales and services organizations are managed through a single CRM technology, with an integrated view of both sales and service automation clouds. We can now predict the forecasting of product and service revenue by monitoring sales lifecycle (pipeline, best case and committed stages) markers and changes to these markers as sales opportunities move from the "pipeline" stage to "best case" stage to the "commit" stage. We do this with automated work flows and cross-functional alerts to best align businesses with real time deal status to optimize operations.

There are different stages in our sales forecast that represent the confidence level for each deal that is actively being managed by our sales teams. This confidence level represents the belief that the sales teams will win the respective business in the current financial quarter. There are various lifecycle markers that are visible to our sales organization and our company as a whole as we're managing the forecast through our CRM system. With the social collaboration tool, Chatter, embedded within the CRM, we have developed the capability where any modification to the forecast is chatted automatically, by the CRM solution, not the sales personnel, as either a positive trajectory or a negative trajectory for a sales opportunity. A simple chat message informs our senior leadership of positive and negative movement in our forecast.

Of course, we don't want to inundate our organization with constant chats about all forecasts. Our executives are only interested in making sure we're engaged on the bigger deals, so we have created filters which trigger chats on only opportunities that fulfill certain parameters. We receive these chat messages in real time—just like you would receive a tweet in real time—and we have the ability to action these messages with a "like" button. If, for example, the CEO clicks "like" on a chat message saying that an opportunity just moved from the "best case" to the "commit" stage, the salesperson involved knows that the CEO is recognizing the effort involved in that movement.

Conversely, if the forecast moves in the negative direction, it's important to remember that the chat functionality should never be viewed as "Big Brother." Trust comes from competence and intentions; the intention of having real-time visibility into forecasting does not mean that if a deal is moving in a negative direction the CEO and his direct reports will now try to micromanage the salesperson to help them win it. There's certainly a natural inclination for us, as leaders, to want to get involved, especially on big opportunities, but because of our culture of customer support and teamwork, we typically offer to collaborate with just a simple question, "How can we help?" We've always told our front line employees, "If you are fighting the battle alone and you're not leveraging the company to help you win, you're not taking part in our collaborative culture."

Leadership is example. Leadership is about accessibility and a willingness to support the team win. As leaders, we have to demonstrate that when you tap us on the shoulder and ask for help, we will be enthusiastically engaged in helping you delight the customer. However, if you ask for help and instead receive a slap on the hand, we know that you'll start to feel defensive about making any changes in the deal status in Salesforce.com's CRM system because you will worry about how the leadership is viewing you. This is why it's crucial that we do not act like "Big Brother." If you use our technology, and you don't have the underpinnings of a social culture, adoption will be slow, and it will create other problematic behavior within your organization.

Without discipline and rigor, even social collaboration will not yield consistently desired outcomes. As leaders, the first thing we do when we start work in the morning is check the Chatter group summaries of the different groups that we belong to, and it's our practice to hit "like" on some of the positive reports. The regional directors of sales and the salespeople involved in those cases can see that we are noticing their efforts, so it's important that we don't automate this behavior, lest it become impersonal. If we were to hit "like" on every positive report— which would be an easy thing to automate—the sales teams would cease to take it personally.

Our CIOs now receive summary reports of all the machine activity on our network throughout the course of each day. They now have a historical perspective on whether network stability, availability, and security are improving over time. Just this simple level of reporting that describes the network health, or the sales forecast health, and the fact that it's being produced by machines rather than people, is bringing an incredible level of efficiency and relevant, actionable, contextual insight to our business. We'll continue to evolve and determine how much more we can use machines to deliver proactive services to our customers. The beauty of all of this is its unparalleled simplicity. It is so simple and elegant to tweet to your network, have the network process the request and then have it tweet back to you, "I finished, and here are the results."

We're enabling real-time response to business needs anytime, anywhere. With a mobile device and the cloud, it's becoming easier and easier to do our jobs. We're bringing predictable, secure management and control across network infrastructure using popular social media constructs. The fact that the communication is happening on Twitter, Facebook, and Chatter ensures that adoption will not be blocked by any lack of training or understanding. Everyone already understands the user interface; now, it's just a matter of leveraging it for business use. We're removing the guesswork from network management, and making it instant and easy to deploy in an IT environment. It doesn't require new skills, and it takes minimal training. Training is usually a big hurdle when trying to adopt a new technology, but in this scenario, because of the simplicity of the design and usability, it's easy to implement. This is the ideal scenario: intellectual property that's hard to replicate, localizable in terms of language, and has an incredibly simple user experience.

With the advent of ISAAC, and our ability to leverage machine sourced collaboration logic, we have the world's first true social sales forecast where machines communicate changes in our sales management workflow to help us collaborate successfully as a well informed and connected team.

Our use of machine to people and machine to machine social collaboration is at its infancy stage. We have 'sensors' that are helping us better understand real-time events in our sales, services, and customer networks. The processing speed of such information is helping us maintain a level of business agility that is beyond what could have been imagined a few years ago, but the most exciting chapters are yet to come, and we are working on projects that will take the human and machine social networks. We will be delivering intelligence to our customers and employees and emphasizing execution velocity, relevancy, simplicity and the user experience.

To swim in blue oceans you need courage, grit, perseverance, and the desire and vision to do more than others expect of you. There are no lifeguards on duty, and the water looks calm and empty; it is this emptiness that makes us question our direction and desired destination. We wonder if we can make the swim on our own without others to validate our efforts. With collaboration technologies, we can capture the pulse of our network – employees, customers, and partners – and weather the storm of uncertainty with courage and conviction to architect value and innovation.

Sometimes underdogs win because the competition wasn't ready for the new play in the playbook. Underdogs must outsmart and outwork the competition to win, and one way to do that is change the game. There is no safety in the status quo.

Twitter Takeaways

Successful adoption of new technologies and processes is heavily impacted by the user experience.

The ability to simplify and improve the customer experience is a core element of a sustainable growth strategy.

Social CIOs recognize that collaboration and mobility is *not* about technology, it is about a lifestyle.

The future social network graph in the enterprise includes both people and products.

Technology vendors must develop technologies to help reduce the consumption gap and improve customer ROI.

Service organization must use BI and transition from defensive mindset to preemptive, offensive service delivery.

You're not a social business unless your social channels are integrated into your business processes and workflow.

Disruptive innovators constantly challenge their assumptions.

The sign near the blue ocean reads: "welcome, you are alone and there are no lifeguards on duty." #innovation

Customers care about having their problems resolved quickly, regardless of the contact channel.

Leadership is about accessibility and willingness to support the team win. Leadership is conversation.

The future of sales is social forecasting – let social CRM expand your sales organization's reach and influence.

To swim in blue oceans you need courage, grit, perseverance, and the desire to be better.

Better sameness is not innovation.

Dear underdog, if you don't think you can win, you have already lost. Dear CIO, simply keeping the lights on will not afford you a seat at your company's "strategic leadership" table.

Dear #CIO, get to know the #CMO well, because very soon, she will have a bigger technology budget than you.

The future social IT department will manage their network enterprise infrastructure via mobile, social applications.

You may hate gravity, but gravity doesn't care." @claychristensen | Dear #CIO, gravity = social + mobile + cloud.

The purpose of social collaboration is to leverage the genius of the crowd to improve business agility.

CHAPTER EIGHT:

The Future of Social

"A business has to be involving, it has to be fun, and it has to exercise your creative instincts." - @RichardBranson

Social business transformation is a long journey. Nearly three years after our initial start, we are still at the very beginning. So what does the future hold for a social business like ours? There are no case studies or documentation about the future. We can only try to forecast our future social transformation roadmap based on the existing business processes and technology trajectories.

The market is the wind, and we cannot control the wind. What we know for sure is that the only constant is change. Our core values will be our guiding principles that help us navigate change. Social business transformation success depends on the following elements in order of importance: culture, people, process, and technology.

Social businesses will work hard to shift from a transaction-oriented model to an engagement model that is more personalized and context rich. Recognizing that our existing and future customers have voices and choices that are scaled and amplified like no other period in our history, we must leverage technology to help scale our responsiveness and improve business agility

Customers will continue to be more social, mobile, and more connected. In order for businesses to meet the customer demand of hyper-connectivity, and real-time service delivery, they will have to place a stronger emphasis on improving their ability to recruit and retain the very best talent.

A social business must also adopt marketing 2.0 principles that focus on value exchange versus extraction. Traditional marketing is dead and the use of social collaboration and enterprise 2.0 technologies is the only viable path towards growth. As @garyvee said, "if content is king, context is God," and without social technologies, the right context is unachievable.

Businesses also have to architect and define lean processes to enhance their customer experience management capabilities, and improve product and service time-to-market execution velocities. The future of social collaboration will significantly impact all lines of business including human resources (HR), marketing, sales, services, and engineering.

The role human resources in a social business will be immensely important as far as shaping and maintaining the company culture. Businesses must be able to recruit employees that demonstrate the right balance of IQ (intelligence) and EQ (emotional) to participate in social collaboration. The right balance of social aptitude and attitude does not mean hiring only a group of extroverts, but rather, finding employees that exhibit humility and a passion for service. Employees must have an open mind, a beginner's mindset – they must be curious and prejudice-free. A social HR organization will adopt a hunter's mentality, networking proactively to recruit candidates with social currency and influence.

Future of Talent Acquisition – Google is Your Resume

In the social era, our employees have the unprecedented ability to either help or hurt our company's brand. Social collaboration within business enables organizations to have greater visibility into our employee's judgment, influence and shared experiences and knowledge. As Tom Peters said so eloquently, "Brand equals talent." As a social business, you have to be able to recruit and keep the best talent, because today the employee is the brand. Perhaps in the past, only frontline employees in sales and services were best suited to represent the company brand, but with the advent and growth of social media, any employee has the opportunity to be seen or heard.

So how does a company in a social era successfully recruit the very best? Based on our experience the best employees are not looking for work; they're too busy changing the world. , The best talent may have their head down, grinding and producing amazing work but they still find time to be social. They're nose- to-the-grindstone doing their jobs. Some might not even have an updated resume, because deep down they know their next move will either be an internal promotion, or an opportunity offered to them through their existing network of other accomplished and trusted advisors. The good news is that the future employees we want at our company are visible. They are on the web and easy to find. For tomorrow's highly active and social talent, the paper resume is dead and unnecessary. Businesses must be highly engaged with social networks – not just LinkedIn – to connect with likeminded, like-skilled employees. To establish relationships with these potential candidates, companies must establish a brand that represents the companies vibrant culture. Social engagement will help the recruitment efforts. It is a pro-active, hunter-like mentality versus a farming mentality, which will enable a social business to recruit the very best talent – a socially engaged and dynamic employee – into our business.

In general, social collaboration is really about sharing and finding relevant information, ideas and people. Collaboration is about connecting, being interested (first), and being interesting (second). Companies are going to be more and more engaged in social media as a means of identifying talented, passionate, and skilled employees who are willing to share their beliefs and their accomplishments. You can Google any active social media participant and instantly know the good, the bad, and the ugly. This is why it is particularly crucial not to be a "smart jerk" in the social stratosphere. It turns out that talking is better suited than shouting while being social. So be likeable; that's our motto, and it's the "L" in SOCIAL. Your social reputation is the only universal currency you have. You might be an expert in an area, but your reputation is still built on a foundation of dignity and respect. Please remember, your reputation follows you wherever you go.

The trend in social networking, from a human resources perspective, is that recruitment is starting to be about offense rather than defense, with Google standing in as a resume. Your social thumbprint will be what gets you through the door instead of your references. In the future, landing an interview will require more than a polished piece of paper. Your digital currency is your ticket to a job interview.

A recent study showed that the average cost of a bad hire is $50,000 for a small mid-market company. It is very expensive to go through the recruitment process and train someone, only to find out ninety days later that they are not a cultural fit or lack the skills needed for the job. Skill set aside, cultural fit is an important element of successful recruitment. For this reason alone, a candidate's network of peers and their social network graph can be a powerful tool to assess cultural fit. It's easy to detect drift from culture in a social business. When everything is humming along, when you have a well-oiled machine that's social, any deviation or drift from your culture gets amplified. For a wrong hire, it's tough to be part of a social business and lack the requisite core values as guiding principles.

It is also important to understand that you can not only leverage a social network to recruit talent, but also to monitor talent performance and growth potential. Once you have talent on board, the annual performance review becomes a thing of the past—or is at least severely threatened by a crowd sourcing model that constantly measures employee value, and communicates it to an organization on a daily basis. The value of an employee is intrinsically tied to their judgment, experience, and influence. All of these things are measured on a regular basis via the social network within and beyond your company. When someone speaks for or within your company, their voice resonates and is adopted. The loudest ones are the not necessarily those of the change agents. The voices that scale and amplify have the potential to influence change the most. Their potential influence is a major asset to any manager or leader. The fact that we can now measure social currency, which is, perhaps, synonymous with influence, is a powerful thing. Influence allows for the possibility of affecting change without using authority. Here is the cautionary red flag: don't confuse influence with popularity. You can have opinions that are well received and re-stated, but that does not automatically equate to influence.

Annual performance reviews are like dieting once a year and expecting to lose weight. Employees anticipate that annual 30-minute discussion with dread, and employers hope that their feedback will somehow manage that individual for the entire next year. There are certainly some great managers who treat the performance review as a foundational element toward a holistic "see it/say it" mentality, and constantly coach and mentor their charges. In a social business, however, it turns out that your impact on the organization is not only visible to you, but it is also visible to others. When you find someone who has the talent for propagating information that can resonate and stick, it not only builds individual brand awareness, it also motivates the manager to fast track that person to bigger and better projects.

HR is already using social platforms such as LinkedIn to do heavy recruiting. We are constantly getting contacted through LinkedIn by other companies eager to hire us, and we use LinkedIn ourselves to look for talent. As managers looking for talent with a very specific skill set, LinkedIn is a logical place to go, especially when you can so easily find people within your own network who already have a tertiary relationship to you. The more these social networks expand, the heavier the social recruiting process is going to become.

How do businesses keep excellent employees who have all of these great attributes, especially when competitors are easily able to connect? How do businesses keep employees motivated and loyal? We know employees are not motivated by money alone. .The answer is for businesses to provide the right culture. For the new generation of talent, it is about cultivating and promoting a social business culture.

As management, you want everyone to feel like a leader. You want people to feel like they're part of a growing, positive organization, empowered by their jobs to really impact the business. You want them to see that there's a focus in the business, that they can drive the business to its next level, that there's collaboration in everything they do, and, on top of all that, you have to be innovative to keep them interested. That's what keeps people locked in, wanting to contribute to a successful organization. We are happy to say that all of the above characteristics are all a deliberate part of our culture at Enterasys.

If you're a potential recruit, go ahead and throw that paper resume away. We're not interested in talking to your boss from a decade ago. We want to know what your current social network has to say about who you are and what you're capable of. Organizations like Klout, Kred, and Peer-Index are all busy amassing intellectual property that uses algorithms to measure your individual impact in the social world. How does your message resonate through a social network? Some will say that your social media reach is not your true influence as a human, but then again, if you tweet something and it gets re-tweeted by 30,000 other people, you must be saying something interesting. People are listening; it's up to the recruitment capabilities of a social business to determine if that message is a fit for the company's needs and desired objectives.

Social Customer Support

In the service and support space, it's easy to see that future customer contact will be prioritized by social influence. If we have two customers contacting us with the same problem about the same product, all other things being equal, it makes sense for us to prioritize the contact that has a stronger social influence, because their feedback is going to make a bigger impact on our reputation. This is not a science and it's not a hard formula. Instead it's the use of yet another data point to make an informed decision. It is shortsighted for companies to ignore digital influence. The use of social influence, or popularity, maybe a taboo topic for most service practitioners, but there is no logical reason for companies to ignore a person's social network reach or amplification potential.

Most contact centers leverage technology to route customer inquiries to the appropriate skilled service professional – often referred to as automated contact/call distribution, which is based on skilled-based routing. Customers can select the area of interest from a phone menu option or email or web template and their contact is automatically routed. Minimal level logic goes into routing customer contacts by domain expertise. A second level of routing concerns the severity of the issue. A typical scenario of fast path routing is based on a customer's description of the error scenario and business impact, which can lead to a faster escalation path to higher skilled engineers in order to improve service execution velocity, rapid resolution, and recovery service level agreements. It is conceivable that sometime in the future, a customer's social influence could lead to a fast-path contact using similar logic. That being said, the severity of the contact, meaning the negative business impact to the customer, trumps all other metrics, and will always take the highest precedent in terms of vendor priority, regardless of the customer's social influence.

The future of service and support in a social business is a customer using a tablet to initiate a Google+ circle hangout, with several concurrent video streams in a collaborative environment. The video chat can include the customer, a partner, a service professional , and perhaps an engineering lead from R&D. You'll collaborate through a social channel on a live video call., All of this will be captured in your CRM, so you will have the ability to do a post-mortem and understand the customer experience.

Social businesses are businesses that understand that differentiation not only comes through collaboration, but also through understanding your competency. Successful social businesses never outsource their core competency. What happens when a customer can contact you by using their mobile video, at any time, from anywhere?, Are you ready to respond via video after you've decided to outsource your services function and the service agent that your customer can see on the other end is obviously reading a script? With video, it becomes quite obvious when the support person you're talking to doesn't truly understand the complexity of your issues, or the solutions you've deployed in your mission-critical network. Social businesses don't outsource their core competency. In a social business, the ecosystem is connected and the competence and intentions of every player are visible.

Social Sales

Perhaps the biggest impact in business is the opportunity to leverage social collaboration to improve the predictability of sales forecasting, opportunity management, and revenue linearity (recognized revenue as a function of time for a fixed time period). The use of social business intelligence in sales can help us target our messages and interactions with people that have digital influence. When speaking to multiple contacts within an organization, understanding and measuring the contacts social footprint and reach allows us to guide our discussions by targeting our message to the person(s) in the organization that is most likely to influence the sales cycle and the buyers.

We believe it is advantageous for us to review all customer and prospect contacts and maintain an internal database that stack-rank the individuals based on their social reach and influence. By using their digital thumbprints to better understand the mindset and core beliefs of customer contacts, we can improve our ability to personalize our messaging, and we can also improve the contextual quality of our communication. The goal is to connect with, and develop relationships with potential advocates that are able to utilize their influence to amplify our voice within their businesses. This idea has vast implications for the service and sales organizations within any company.

Social sales forecasting, powered by CRM also provides us with a very strong tool to help improve sales forecast management capabilities. Today, we are automating our sales forecast management processes using social collaboration technologies that are integrated into our CRM solution. As sales forecast fields are modified by sales associates, an extended team of stakeholders are automatically notified via social channels. Real-time social sales forecasting extends our ability to collaborate, and improves the likelihood and our ability to win business.

Machine-to-Machine Technology

Continuing with social futures, certainly machine-to-machine collaboration will accelerate service delivery. A true social enterprise is one that includes both people and products in its social graph. At Enterasys, we are leveraging machine-to-machine collaboration in service and support to accelerate the service delivery to our customers. We'll continue to quantify this process with more of a critical eye, but it's at least ten times faster when we remove the human interaction required from the customer to the vendor and simply connect the machines through a social network.

Partner and customer communities are going to flourish in this social ecosystem. From a service and support point of view, social business are going to use the genius of the crowd and extend that beyond their employees to their customer and partner base, so that when a customer machine sends a diagnostic message to a vendor through the social cloud, that cloud will invite other customers and partners. Together, the ecosystem of customer, partner, and technology vendor will be able to leverage each other's domain expertise to troubleshoot, optimize, or further automate and build the most robust enterprise networks using each other's capabilities.

Here's a tangible example of what we're talking about:

Seton Hill University has 3,000 students and faculty connected to their network using Enterasys networking technology. In 2012, Seton Hill's innovative CIO, Phil Komarny agreed to leverage our SaaS CRM solution –Salesforce.com – to connect their enterprise IT staff, and machine networks to our contact center at Enterasys via a public social network. This public social network was powered by Salesforce.com's Chatter solution. Seton Hill now leverages a Chatter social cloud and they've registered their machines as well as their IT employees so that when their machines communicate, the messages are delivered to the IT staff and Enterasys' service and support staff simultaneously, in real time.

The biggest benefit of having social collaboration in a tool that also serves as your contact center ticket system is the ability to transition key data points – social conversations – to the services and ticketing system of our CRM solution. Based on the specific forensics and the message that the machine is producing, we could choose to create automatic service cases, and we often do. If a component fails within a system—for example, if a fan or a power supply in a switcher or a router fails (a common occurrence which fortunately does not hinder the system because there is redundancy built in with multiple fans)—we want to replace it as soon as possible. When an item fails, we receive a message through our social cloud from the machine itself. Because the message comes in through Salesforce.com's native chat functionality and a service ticket can be created immediately, a new fan is processed and shipped immediately, and all of this is done automatically without any human intervention. Universal machine-to-machine collaboration through social networking is a guaranteed inevitability.

As we mentioned in chapter three, Ford and Toyota have been early adopters of this idea of machine-to-machine serviceability through a social network. In the near future, when you have a flat tire, your car will automatically notify the nearest roadside assistance company, tow truck, or the dealer from where you bought the car. You'll have the ability, in advance, to configure your car's system to choose who gets notified in each situation, and help will be on the way before you can call AAA. If you're the kind of person who really likes to change your own tire by the side of the road, you'll have the option of replying to the network with "Never mind, I'm good," but having to scroll through your phone contact list or scrambling to find your AAA card will be a thing of the past. Billions of cars are going to be networked in an ecosystem that will bring massive efficiency to the driver experience. We have built a social ecosystem that connects our customers and business partners to us with real-time visibility of enterprise network operations. What the auto industry is attempting to build exists at Enterasys today.

A World of Free Advice

One benefit social tools already give us is the ability to extract information that previously required access to an industry analyst. Today, however, we live in an information sharing economy, which means the very analysts that used to be protected by their firm's walls are now willingly sharing though open social networks. As we noted earlier, trust is established by the combination of competence and intentions. In the social era, the intentions must be clear: sharing is how we bolster our social currency.

The fact is we don't need people to just bring us new ideas without the ability to help with the execution and understanding of business alignment. Ideas are everywhere, but resources are not. We need talented people that can execute relevant ideas. Ideas relevant to whom, you ask? Ideas must be relevant to our employees, and beneficial to our customers and business partners. We can harness the best ideas in the world about leadership, but without execution, they are meaningless. We don't look for consultants; we look for people who can help us make our strategy a reality.

Given the fact that, in the social era, everyone has the opportunity to influence – due to the unprecedented scale and amplification of voice enabled by social media – the analyst landscape is subject to dramatic change. The other element is the speed of innovation. Analysts no longer have years, or decades to hone their views. In the social enterprise and networking industry, some of the fastest growing and adaptive companies are less than a year old. The open nature of knowledge sharing and the scale of individuality will challenge our traditional view of industry analysts and pundits.

Today, we notice that most analysts are shifting from using 'best practice' terminology to 'considered practice.' Is this to protect their thought leadership and intellectual capital given the speed of innovation, success and failure? Perhaps, but the main challenge will be finding patterns that are consistent throughout markets given the diverse use and implementation models of modern, digital transformation initiatives. The days when a consultant or an analyst would ask for your watch and then tell you the time, so to speak, are long gone.

The speed of innovation and the velocity of technology evolution in multiple dimensions are challenging Moore's law, which states that the amount of computer processing power effectively doubles over a certain period of time (typically 2 years). The details of this are best left for true geeks like us, but, in a nutshell, what this means is that people no longer have the need upgrade constantly. There used to be a time when you had to habitually update your PC in order to keep it functioning well.

Now, instead, we throw our machines and devices away after a few years because there is something newer, faster, and better. Apple, for example, has really capitalized on this concept.

Similarly, social media is exploding so quickly that it's hard to keep track; some of the fastest growing social networks did not exist 12 months ago, which shows that the growth and popularity of web-based service companies are unpredictable and potentially explosive as well. Social networks and apps pop up every day, and hundreds of millions of users adopt them. Some survive, others won't.

The Social Impact on Products

No longer will engineering companies say to marketing, "Let me build a product, and then you can go find a customer for it." That's dumb and expensive. A lot of high tech companies still operate this way: they build what they're good at, and when the product doesn't sell, they complain that they need better marketing or better partners. What they actually need to be doing is solving real problems with solutions that customers want. In the future, crowd sourcing will drive engineering. Any time you produce a product, whether it's a tangible product or a service product, or deliver a monetized solution, you'll use crowd sourcing techniques to get an early understanding of whether it's going to resonate with the market.

How do you incentivize customers and partners to be part of your innovation engine? In order to foster mass collaboration, you have to treat it like a game. Create a target behavior and mindset, score the mindset along the way, recognize the individuals who are achieving according to your desired outcome, and design the principle so that people understand they're contributing value to the process.

Businesses need to change. Businesses are popping up out of nowhere. We have markets that are shutting down and starting up literally within less than a year. It is important to ensure your resources are providing the best value to the business. So as we crowd source ideas, there's going to be constant socialization of those ideas, and constant reflection back to the community, which will allow us to check in: "is this what you need?" This is a drastic departure from current tactic, which involves tasking marketing with a requirements document that then goes back to R&D. Instead, there will be a much more collaborative process of developing products in tandem with the customer.

The Ultimate Payoff of a Transparent Culture

Once again we come back to the idea of an absolutely transparent culture. Companies that are more transparent are going to get more business, period. Even today, when we select vendors, we look for those who are willing to put all of their information on the cloud so that we can see their data up front, from there we can choose their products based on what they say the products will do, how they can prove it, and how we see the products performing in real time. Businesses willing to put themselves out there in this way create the credibility to build trust in all aspects of their business. We already have cloud-hosted databases where we can post our product performance results. Conversely, we have our component vendors using the same tools to post their product performance information, which allows us to select their particular product lots and express exactly what we want from them. In this way, vendors are offering data that is truly transparent, which allows us, as their customer, to make selections based on complete information. This kind of vendor transparency is groundbreaking, because, historically the big vendors have kept their data locked up and behind closed doors.

Being transparent drives a social currency of value to the end customer. At Enterasys, we provide our customers with a tremendous amount of product data, we let them know how we perform, and encourage them to compare us on merit. In actuality, this is not all too different from the concept of Angie's List or Yelp, where customers review online ratings of products and experiences so as to make informed purchasing or patronizing decisions. The high degree of transparency and accountability drives business continuity and performance, and thus crowd sourcing becomes an opportunity for any social business to take advantage of the invaluable wisdom customers can provide.

A social business crowd sources, and it also embraces gaming principles to improve business performance. Gamification is not about having fun or playing games; it's about achieving business results through engaged employees, customers, and partners. There's no question that engaged employees equal productive employees. How do you effectively motivate your team, your customer, or your partners? How do you get people to use your processes, or be part of your innovation engine? Competition can be a great internal driver. It's important to keep score. Given the rules of the game, who's winning? Which partner has submitted the most product enhancement requests that have gone on to development? Which customer is using your product in the most innovative way?

Foursquare, for example, has their own unique scorecard, and it's incredibly effective. It encourages people to "check in" at physical locations as they go about their day. When you check in at Dunkin' Donuts the most times, you become virtual "Mayor." It's a silly little badge, but people are competitive about it. A-players really want to win.

There is no point in tracking partner or employee activity and successes if you're not going to recognize them down the line. Simply communicating achievement can be recognition enough,   but   for a customer, a social business also gives tangible rewards for recognition, such as product discounts. Customers that are a part of the collaborative ecosystem should be promoted publicly.

Integration of Social Interface and Tools

We have been working for a number of years to cultivate a culture of collaboration, investing time into developing and defining leaner processes, business intelligence and reporting, and value-added services. This cultivating work has helped us foster a rich ecosystem of shared accountability that extends beyond our company – to partners and customers. The first paragraph of this book states that winning is best when it is shared with customers and partners. That being said, our aim is to develop technology that can help our customers and partners become a social business. We believe that real social collaboration drives significant user benefits.

We are developing applications that enable us to better understand the usage of web applications, including social networking applications, which provide visibility into specific profiles that help us better understand the adoption of technology, through both functional groups and specific users. We can then index application usage by popularity, which gives us the ability to either promote additional training for improved adoption or to modify governance in order to optimize our business continuity and productivity. The levels of social intelligence instrumentation that we can incorporate into our business workflow and products will grow increasingly over time. A social interface will expand our forensics-gathering capabilities from internal business application basis (an example being a social CRM network of users), and expand to external channels that include a network of customers, business partners, and component vendors.

For us, ISAAC is an example of a mobile, social, cloud-based monitoring and management tool. But our vendors are doing social things with their own tools too, which makes it much easier for us to resource our engineers in a more effective way. In the future, our engineers are going to bring ideas to market much faster. There's already an ability to collaborate with tools, and now they're going to be collaborating outside of their environments, going beyond user groups, and proactively engaging when there are user group communities through social avenues that can benefit from their use of a particular tool. This is all just beginning.

The cloud has enabled so many innovations, and it is now tremendously easy to collaborate globally. We have many examples, in our own business of cloud-enabled tools, which allow us to quickly and easily access vendors, whether they are in Romania or Thailand. That kind of collaboration, over the next several years, is going to take another next step: proactive engagements will not only target the people that are out there helping us bring our products to market, they will also use the tools and the machinery itself. The machinery and the tools today have static feeds; tomorrow those are going to be dynamic social feeds back into our business—entire groups can know exactly what the factory yields are, and can understand how well each product is progressing in the production process. What are the issues that require us to solicit engineering or customer input? Social integration is about to enter the product development cycle on a whole new level, and it will eliminate a great deal of human delay out of that cycle.

Social Marketing and Brand Scale

Marketing is a key area in the future of social. Inbound marketing and content creation will be valuable investments in terms of social media training. The biggest ally that marketing will have will be found in the collective employee voice. This will be how marketing will scale and bring a human voice to the business, but first, marketing departments will have to adopt the ethos of value exchange, not just value extraction. It's not a one-way conversation; if you're only using social media to propagate your press release, you're not social. Remember: it's a telephone, not a megaphone. You have to have reciprocal conversations with your customers and your partners.

We work for at a small to medium size company, but we have nearly 20,000 global customers. If one of our customers tweets something about us, we answer that tweet, and we provide said customer with what she needs. The notion of "spray and pray content" is gone in the social era. There is no other way other than to utilize employee empowerment in order to best scale and humanize your enterprise. It starts with recruiting and training social employees, and then getting them to be a natural extension of your marketing organization.

Social analytics, which can be used by marketers to build brand advocates, provide a good example of brand promotion. A personal example of this is how the hospitality industry is listening. They are using social networks to find ways to improve the customer experience. These days, when we travel, we make a habit of tweeting about the hotel we're going to be staying at just before we check in. Nine times out of ten, this results in an upgrade provided by the hotel. Of course, this is not happening just because we are sending one optimistic tweet about the hotel stay, it's happening because whoever is reading that tweet is doing the legwork to look into who we are, using social analytic tools like Klout, and finding out just how powerful our social reach is. The hotel is betting that, if they upgrade us, the world will hear about how much we love them. And it works! That's how the social game is played. It's an ethos of value exchange, and the strongest tool we have in our arsenal is our ability to be advocates.

Blogging is going to be a significant element in the future of social. You have to be able to extend a relationship beyond a 140 character tweet, or a Facebook wall post. Producing content that's valuable and relevant through blogs and micro blogs is one way to impart more information to your customers and partners without spamming them. IBM has 440,000 employees and 70,000 contractors, and they have 40,000 active bloggers who participate in 70,000 communities. A recent MIT-Sloan post discussed the vibrant community of IBM. How does a one hundred-year-old, half-a-million-employee company participate successfully in social? By empowering and investing in their employees.

We believe that the next wave in blogging will be video blogs. In our service organization, we are currently converting all of our knowledge-base solutions to video blogs. We have 10,000 published solutions, so it's a big project, and it was a challenge to figure out how to most efficiently meet this task. Every day, we have every single one of our employees produce a short, two to three minute video. They take a recommendation, break it into small components, and make sure that the customer can pinpoint exactly what they need at any particular point in the video. If a picture is worth a thousand words, a video is worth a hundred thousand words. When a video can convey the exact intricacies of how to manage and troubleshoot a situation, it becomes an invaluable customer tool. More importantly, when a customer realizes that you have intelligence automated in your arsenal in this way, it's a value-add service. To make our service even more functional and enticing, we include a pop-up message that says "Hi, my name is Brad. I'm an expert in this area. If you have any questions that are not answered by this video, let us have a video chat right now." The customer's experience is painless and seamless. They gain access to a vast library of video blogs, with the added option of instant human connection. Video is going to play a massive role in connecting customers and enterprises in the future. Facetime and Skype are already wildly popular mediums through which people can connect around the globe. These days, when we travel, we don't even think about using the phone. It's just so easy to start a video call on a mobile device or computer. In our offices in Boston, there is video conferencing equipment that connects us securely to thirty offices around the world. Over time the traditional use of phone may become practically obsolete as a way for us to communicate internally. Instead, instant mobile video conferencing, powered by social collaboration tools will be the preferred communication channel.

When it really comes down to it, the nature of being a social business is all about intimacy and forming human connections. The future of marketing is community building, which will be done through video, blogs, chatting features, social media. Marketing to one person is an important mindset that every social business must adopt and scale.

Winning Together

Social collaboration in business flattens hierarchies. Ideas are like sound, traveling throughout the seams of our organizational social fabric in all directions. Our ability to influence our peers and other lines of business will scale, given the culture of ultra-transparency that will exist in business. The level of transparency is also extended outside of the company, whereby customers and business partners will work together, governed by the collective ethos of value exchange, instead of an ethos of extraction. The purpose of co-creation will improve our ability to truly understand our employee and customer needs.

The promise of social collaboration is that best ideas will win. Ideas need light, air, and nourishment in order to flourish into actionable results. In a social business, ideas—not titles—win. The ultimate goal, of a true social business, is that of a "leaderless" organization, wherein mass collaboration produces the desired objectives. Managers will always lead companies, and hierarchies will always exist, but there is a 'softening' effect of this vertical construct in a social business. Today, employees that work in a truly social business are comfortable engaging with the C-suite, including the CEO. At our company, employees talk to our executive management; we use each other's names; we eat lunch together and have meaningful conversations to grow our business. Leadership is developed through conversation, and, in a social business, conversations are vibrant and extensive.

We are only at the beginning or our social business transformation journey. We know that social collaboration has helped democratize our business and markets by giving us the opportunity to share what we believe with our communities. We are a world-class company that, for 30 years, has delivered outstanding products and services to our amazing customers around the globe. We are a great company to work for, as has been recognized by our customers, partners, the press, and business analysts alike. We are a social business that fosters collaboration and sharing in order to bring meaning to our personal and professional lives. The best marketing today is to care more, and a social business lives by— thrives by—promoting an ethos of caring. Ultimately, we don't think of ourselves as underdogs because we are not driven by comparisons. That being said, we do believe we are the right size business because we have a reputation of consistently delivering on our promises.

We win, because we know we can. We win because we care. We win because we are social. Our hope is that you will learn from our story. We hope that you can win, compete and grow your market share by adopting a social collaboration strategy. Let us know how we can help.

Thank you.

@ValaAfshar and @Brad_W_Martin

Twitter Takeaways

Social businesses work hard to make every transaction feel like an engagement. You matter.

Existing and future customers have voices and choices that are scaled and amplified like no other period in our history.

Social businesses recruit employees that demonstrate balance of IQ (intelligence) and EQ (emotional intelligence).

Social collaboration enables organizations to have greater visibility of our employees' judgment, influence and knowledge

As a social business, you have to be able to recruit and keep the best talent, because today, the employee is the brand.

For tomorrow's highly active social talent, the paper resume is dead and unnecessary. Google is your resume.

Social collaboration is about sharing, finding, connecting, being interested (first), and being interesting (second).

It is particularly crucial not to be a "smart jerk" in the social stratosphere. Negativity is amplified.

Your reputation must be built on a foundation of dignity and respect. Your reputation follows you wherever you go.

Social business employees know they're part of a growing, positive organization, and that they can impact the business

In the social era, the intentions must be clear: sharing is how we bolster our social currency.

A social business has talented people that can execute against relevant ideas that matter to community.

Transparency leads to trust and mutual respect. A culture of transparency will fuel business growth. Period.

Customers that are a part of the collaboration ecosystem should be promoted publicly

The marketing notion of "spray and pray content" is gone in the social era.

A social business' values are based on the ethos of value exchange, not value extraction.

How do companies of all sizes participate successfully in social? By empowering and investing in their employees.

A social business must work hard to earn a reputation by consistently delivering on their promises.

We win, because we know we can. We win because we care. We win because we are social.

REFERENCES

Armano, David. On Social Media Becoming Social Business. HBR Blog Network, 2011. Available at: http://blogs.hbr.org/cs/2011/07/on_social_media_becoming_socia.html. Accessed July 2012.

Blacharski, Dan. "Closing the consumption gap: Making use of the features you have." ITWorld, 2012. Available at: http://www.itworld.com/it-managementstrategy/292984/closing-consumption-gap-making-use-features-you-have. Accessed September 2012.

Bradley, Anthony & Mark McDonald. All Organizations Are Social, But Few Are Social Organizations. HBR Blog Network, 2011. Available at: http://blogs.hbr.org/cs/2011/10/all_organizations_are_social_b.html. Accessed July 2012.

Branson, Richard. "A business has to be involving, it has to be fun, and it has to exercise your creative instincts. – @richardbranson #business-quote." Twitter, 2012. Retrieved from https://twitter.com/MidMarketUK/status/241098397451436032

Clayton Christensen. BrainyQuote.com, Xplore Inc, 2012. http://www.brainyquote.com/quotes/authors/c/clayton_christensen.html.   Accessed September 099, 2012.

Comaford, Christine. "If You Aren't Social, You'll Shrink: 10 Steps To Becoming a Social Business." Forbes, 2012.Available at: http://www.forbes.com/sites/christinecomaford/2012/06/19/if-you-are-not-social-you-will-shrink-10-steps-to-becoming-a-social-business/.   Accessed July 2012]

Cuban, Mark. BrainyQuote.com, Xplore Inc, 2012. http://www.brainyquote.com/quotes/authors/m/mark_cuban.html. Accessed September 099, 2012.

Feldman, Mark. "Did This Security Company's Use of Social Media Just Pass the Turing Test?" Forbes, 2012. Available at: http://www.forbes.com/sites/markfidelman/2012/07/09/did-this-security-companys-use-of-social-media-just-pass-the-turing-test/ Accessed July 2012.

Ford, Henry. Strategicbusiness.com, 2012. http://www.strategicbusinessteam.com/famous-small-business-quotes/henry-fords-quotes-famous-business-and-leadership-quotes-from-an-automobile-billionaire-industrialist-and-one-of-the-richest-men-ever-in-history/. Accessed September 9, 2012.

Godin, Seth. Goodreads.com, 2012. http://www.goodreads.com/quotes/152953-change-almost-never-fails-because-it-s-too-early-it-almost. Accessed September 9, 2012.

Kim, Chan & Renee Mauborgne, "Blue Ocean Strategy: How to Create Uncontested Market Space and Make Competition Irrelevant", Harvard Business School Press, 2005.

Kiron, David & Jeff Schick. "How IBM Builds Vibrant Social Communities." MIT Sloan Management Review, 2012. Available at: http://sloanreview.mit.edu/feature/how-ibm-builds-vibrant-social-communities/. Accessed July 2012.

Levie, Aaron. The Simplicity Thesis. Fast Company, 2012. Available at: http://www.fastcompany.com/1835983/simplicity-thesis. Accessed September 2012.

McAfee, Andrew. What Sells CEOs on Social Networking. MIT Sloan Management Review, 2012. Available at: http://sloanreview.mit.edu/feature/what-sells-ceos-on-social-networking/, Accessed July 2012.

Peters, Tom. BrainyQuote.com, Xplore Inc, 2012. http://www.brainyquote.com/quotes/authors/t/tom_peters.html accessed September 099, 2012.

Peters, Tom. BrainyQuote.com, Xplore Inc, 2012. http://www.brainyquote.com/quotes/authors/t/tom_peters.html. Accessed September 099, 2012.
Peters, Tom. Strategy: Excellence: Brand Equals Talent. TomPeters.com, 2009. Available at: http://www.tompeters.com/blogs/toms_

videos/2009/10/61strategybrand_equals_talent.html.   Accessed September 2012.

Robbins, Tony. BrainyQuote.com, Xplore Inc. http://www.brainyquote.com/quotes/authors/t/tony_robbins_2.html. Accessed September 099, 2012.

Sinek, Simon. Start with Why, Available at: http://www.startwithwhy.com/Read.aspx. Accessed September 2012.

Sinek, Simon. "Transparency doesn't mean sharing every detail. Transparency means providing context for the decisions we're make." Twitter, 2012. Retrieved from https://twitter.com/simonsinek/status/240076801639084032

Twain, Mark. BrainyQuote.com, Xplore Inc., 2012. http://www.brainyquote.com/quotes/authors/m/mark_twain_8.html.   Accessed September 099, 2012.

Vaynerchuk, Gary. Bill Faeth, 2012. If content is king, than context is god. Business2Community, 2012. Available at http://www.business-2community.com/content-marketing/gary-vaynerchuk-if-content-is-king-than-context-is-god-0270374#KbVRFhYfFZG9s2I0.99. Accessed September 2012]

Welch, Jack. Goodreads.com, 2012. http://www.goodreads.com/quotes/185636-if-the-rate-of-change-on-the-outside-exceeds-the. Accessed September 9, 2012.

Wooden, John. Goodreads.com. http://www.goodreads.com/quotes/175299-being-average-means-you-are-as-close-to-the-bottom. Accessed September 9, 2012.

Wood, J.B. - Complexity Avalanche – Overcoming The Threat to Technology Adoption, by J.B. Wood, 2009, Point B Inc, page 6. Wood, JB. "Consumption Gap"

BIOS

Vala Afshar is the Chief Customer Officer for Enterasys Network, a Siemens Enterprise Communications company. He started his career at Enterasys in 1996 as a part-time student while studying for his graduate degree at the University of Massachusetts. Vala was a member of the engineering organization for 10 years and was promoted to Vice President of Software and Hardware Quality Assurance and Solutions Engineering. In 2006, Vala was asked to expand his role and responsibilities to be more customer facing.

At that point, Vala became responsible for global services and support functions at Enterasys. He had an opportunity to be part of, and collaborate with, various functions within the company— R&D, professional and educations services, sales, supply chain, marketing, finance, services—and, over time was afforded the opportunity to serve as the company's first Chief Customer Officer. As the CCO, Vala is responsible for ensuring that every decision made in the company is in the best interests of the customer. Vala's presiding philosophy has always been that "customer success is key," and this is a cornerstone of his work with Enterasys. Vala has been instrumental in ensuring that this attitude is a part of the company's DNA and ethos: "there is nothing more important than our customers," and that includes your "internal customers," or employees.

Brad Martin is the Vice President of Quality and Engineering Operations for Enterasys Networks. Martin has been with Enterasys for over twelve years, and started with the company by working as a summer co-op during engineering school. Martin graduated from the University of Maine in 1998 with a degree in mechanical engineering, and initially went to work for another company upon graduation. He came back to Enterasys in 2000 as an Engineering Manager, expanded his engineering responsibilities, and was eventually promoted to Vice President of Engineering Operations. In 2009 Martin took responsibility for Enterasys hardware quality assurance, and has since assumed responsibility for all quality functions at Enterasys including Software Quality, Hardware Quality, Customer Quality and Quality Management Systems. Martin sits on "Manufacturing Executive Magazine's" Executive Leadership Council, and his teams were awarded two ML100 awards in 2012 for achievement in Quality and Culture.

Both Vala and Brad became Vice Presidents at Enterasys at the age of 33 after being promoted more than a dozen times each. They now report to the Chief Executive Officer of Enterasys, and collectively oversee engineering operations, quality assurance, customer engagement, and the global quality footprint. They have won individual awards, had numerous white papers written about their methodologies, and are lauded as the voices of the social enterprise future by various prestigious publications and analyst groups. They are considered to be industry leaders in quality, service, and support.